sistering

SISTERING

The Art of Holding Close and Letting Go

Jessica Dickey and Danielle Neff

the pilgrim press

The Pilgrim Press, 1300 East 9th Street
Cleveland, Ohio 44114
thepilgrimpress.com

© 2023 Jessica Dickey and Danielle Neff

Photo credits: Authors' private collection, p. iii, p. 1, p. 47; Emily Schriver, p. 143

All rights reserved. No part of this book may be used or reproduced in any manner whatsoever without written permission.

Published 2023.

Except in the case of family members, for the sake of privacy/anonymity, all names have been changed.

Printed on acid-free paper.

Library of Congress Cataloging-in-Publication Data on file.
LCCN: 2022946399

ISBN 978-0-8298-0005-0 (paper)
ISBN 978-0-8298-0006-7 (ebook)

Printed in the United States of America.

FOR MOM AND DAD
the Bald and the Beautiful

Contents

❁

PART ONE: **BEGINNINGS**

Being There ⋯ 3

First Memory ⋯ 6

How We Got Here ⋯ 10

Wildflowers and Cut Grass ⋯ 16

Tuesday Mornings ⋯ 22

When We Get Stuck ⋯ 28

Church Makes Me Cry ⋯ 32

Funerals and Goodbyes ⋯ 39

❁

PART TWO: **BODIES**

When I Didn't Answer ⋯ 49

Unanswered Calls ⋯ 62

Her Body Told Me ⋯ 66

People Know about My Body ⋯ 76

Babies ⋯ 93

Not a Mother ⋯ 101

The Fence ⋯ 106

The Gate ⋯ 115

Unconditional Positive Regard ⋯ 119

I Didn't Tell Her ⋯ 123

Divorce Is ⋯ 131

My Ovaries Don't Work ⋯ 136

❀

PART THREE: **BENEDICTIONS**

Sense of Place ⋯ 145

Trust in the World ⋯ 153

Bringing Liam to a Deathbed ⋯ 159

Brimming with the Sacred ⋯ 168

Pineapple Man ⋯ 175

What if We Get Cancer (And Other Possible Endings) ⋯ 183

Benedictions ⋯ 189

PART ONE

beginnings

BEING THERE

~ ✿ ~

Jessie

I remember lying on a kid-sized picnic table in the living room. The back of the house, a tall, narrow Victorian perched precariously near an active railroad track. This is Marion, Pennsylvania, a hamlet of a few hundred people. *The Wizard of Oz* is on the little TV screen. I lie on my stomach, my elbows digging into the wooden picnic table, my hands digging into my chin—a tripod steadying my unblinking gaze at the object of my fascination—*the Wicked Witch of the West*. Who is she? Why is she so mad? She has an army of monkeys. She has a castle. She has exceptional transportation. So what's the problem?

I remember a pair of legs in striped stockings, jutting out from under the clapboard house. This was her sister, the Wicked Witch of the East. Dorothy's tornado-tumbled house killed her, and her sister of the West wants to know who did it. (She also wants those killer red heels.) No one ever talks about that—*The Wizard of Oz* is launched for the revenge of a slain sister.

A few years later and a few miles down the road, in another house, another hamlet (Waynesboro, Pennsylvania), I remember climbing the stairs and shyly pushing open a closed door, my face peering into the moist bedroom dark. My mother is sitting in a rocking chair, one leg in her nylons, one leg out. She is crying. She is worried about money.

I remember climbing pine trees all the way to the top. I remember burying seashells in the ground below the pine trees. I remember taking nail polish from a neighbor's house. I remember walking a mile and a half to school. I loved those walks. The transition from home self to social self. I remember being pushed down the stairs by a boy that liked me. I remember getting glasses. How exotic and expensive they were. I remember showing my face now marred with glasses to this aggressive boy, thinking, *This will show him*. I turned around at my desk, like *Behold! I am ugly now!* As if that would give me power. He received my meaning. Later that day he pushed me down the stairs.

I remember needing another pair of glasses the very next year. Then another. Then another. Every year. I liked frames that were blue, then red, always bold, even as I grew more and more ashamed of the expense. Of my medical liability. I remember sitting with my face to the oculus instrument, wringing my hands, a test on which I could not get an A+.

I remember many bowls of cereal—magic because no one was counting how much you had. As opposed to the dinner table, when I remember gauging the amount of food on the table and the amount on people's plates, whether it was okay to take a little more.

I remember mud pies. Dinner bells. Bats in the attic. Bats in the bedrooms. Bats in the summer dusk, kamikaze above whiffle ball games. I remember sitting on the front porch to watch thunderstorms, the lightning and wind making the trees alive. I remember the smell of our pet sheepdog.

I do not remember when there was Dani.

I cannot remember her *being there*. Or *not being there*. She just was.

There are stories about this transition, the typical sibling adjustment to a new rung on the ladder. But even if my mind tells me she could not have been there when I watched the Wicked Witch of the West on the picnic table, I was too little, she was not born yet, I remember her being there. Or the *feeling* of her being there. As if she always was. As if the only way I can remember something is if it has with it the feeling of Dani being there. Maybe it was me who was not there until *she* was there. I didn't exist until Dani was there to see me. Her little legs were jutting out. But instead of dying, she was arriving. I mounted my broom and wagged my crooked finger at everyone. I shouted and swished my dress. But instead of her legs disappearing under the house, we made a billow of red smoke. We made fire. She climbed onto my broom.

And up we went.

FIRST MEMORY

Dani

My phone dings. I look down to find a text from my sister, Jessie. It's a picture of her reflection in a mirror, a selfie she has taken from a dressing room. She's wearing something akin to a potato sack with buttons. She has styled it with booties and a wide-brimmed hat. She looks effortlessly cool.

"How's it feel to be in the demographic that wears Eileen Fisher?" I quip back.

She texts me back an emoji crying from laughter and responds.

"Old and smelling like patchouli? You're a skank. But really, what do you think?"

"I think it's annoying how good that looks. I like it. But really, get out of there, my train is pulling in."

I send her back a selfie on the train.

I arrive in New York Penn Station, and across a beehive of people buzzing about their day, I spot her and everything in my body relaxes a little. She sees me and we weave towards one another and embrace.

I have this feeling every morning at 8:20 when I call my sister after dropping my daughter Grace off at daycare, but these few days in New York with her will be the long form version of those phone calls. For the next forty-eight hours, we will do nothing in particular except eat Indian food and Haagen-Dazs ice cream with Oreos. We'll shop and get a pedicure. We'll encourage each other to indulge. We'll binge watch *Game of Thrones*. And we will talk about anything and everything. It is heaven.

My earliest memory is in our old house. Not the old house where I spent the better part of my childhood, but the old, old house. The old house that my parents bought *before* the current old house. I'm at the bottom of the staircase, looking up. The stairs are painted blue, and at the top of them, my sister stands. Shiny blond hair with tragic bowl-cut bangs, pink corduroys, and a Care-Bear t-shirt. I'm two, she's five. She's willing me to climb up those perilous steps. Coaxing me to risk the fall to get up there to be with her.

It seems impossible that I would remember something from that early in my life and yet this is the way it is with so many of my memories, a snapshot, a gesture, bright blue eyes ablaze with a shared secret. My whole life is filled with memories like this: tea parties in the middle of the night, hot summer nights sweating in the same bed but not wanting to separate, lying on the big bed watching her do her hair. Sharing the bathroom, I'm sitting on the toilet seat yammering on while Jessie is shampooing. "Switch," she calls out, and now we've switched places, the conversation continuing. Now she's on the toilet seat and I'm shampooing, the mirrors fogging from the shower-go-round.

There are only a few times we hear about sisters in the Bible and one of them is the story of Rachel and Leah. An unfortunate narrative where two sisters end up married to the same man. Sometimes, I wonder about those sisters, Rachel and Leah. Did they curl up together at night and share stories? Did they take turns giving back rubs? Before the story got twisted through the eyes and actions of Jacob, what closeness did these sisters share? If we had known the story through their eyes, would we have seen the bitterness between sisters the story implies? Or would we have seen something deeper and more nuanced? A story of sisters whose lives and futures were bound up with one another in ways far more important and deeper than any husband? I wonder what story God was already telling through them? What story did God continue to tell that didn't get printed?

I imagine them huddled together, gleeful for their time in the "red tent" when they could cackle together and eat obscene amounts of hummus. I imagine them holding each other when a baby was lost, humming quietly and murmuring comfort. I like to think of them smiling at how clever they are.

The steadiness in how I stand in the world is due in large part to my sister's existence, a safety net moving with me, ready to break a fall. But it's more than that. I can feel that I steady her in the world, too. My sister sees me as more than I am, or maybe she just believes in me more than I say them out loud. She is the person who hears my ideas and longings and convictions, sometimes even before I do. I know that the calling in my life to serve and speak was put there by God, but so was my relationship with Jessie. I would dare to say that she's the reason that I found my voice. She's the one who called it out of me. The reason I have a voice is because my whole life, I had someone who made me feel like I was worth listening to, worth being with. From the moment I was born she was reaching out to me, bringing me along, calling me up, pushing me ahead, reminding me that I could do it. I could be it. I could say it. I could share it. And she would be with me every step of the way.

HOW WE GOT HERE

Jessie

Our parents moved to our hometown of Waynesboro, Pennsylvania as young, poor hippies. They lived on Little Africa Lane. They had a pet skunk named Flower Power. Barry Dickey would become a gym teacher in the elementary system; Sarie Dickey would become a social worker for the Franklin/Fulton County mental health system. In their fifty plus years of marriage, they would earn the nickname The Bald and The Beautiful. They would have many pets. And crappy cars. And three children.

When the pandemic hit, like many loved ones, Dani and I were separated. She was in Pennsylvania, holding down a fort of three children and a congregation of four hundred; I was in Los Angeles for a gig and then in France with my partner. Dani and I had never gone more than three months without seeing each other. This separation would last a year and a half.

So we decided to write a book. (That's just logic, right?) But Dani and I have always shared our writing. In Dani's years as a pastor, she has preached hundreds of sermons—none without first being read by me. In my career as a playwright, premiering plays in New York and around the country, Dani has been my first reader. She's the person I talk it out with, who helps me brainstorm, who lets me bitch, who yelps when I have a victory. By supporting each other's writing, we have supported each other's most authentic expression of self. We've done this through heartache, trauma, marriage, divorce, children, across continents, and through a pandemic.

The internet tells me that a sermon is a talk on a religious or moral subject, especially one given during a church service and based on a passage from the Bible. The internet also tells me that a play is a dramatic work for the stage or to be broadcast.

Neither sounds very interesting.

And yet all over the world, hundreds of thousands of people devote time and resources to hearing both. Why? Because at their core, listening to a sermon and listening to a play are essentially the same—a moment separated from daily life (by environment, by pageantry, by ritual)—built through an intellectual argument to arrive at a spiritual truth. A resonant nugget to carry back into regular life.

Now let me be clear: I'm an agnostic. At *best*. I don't like church. I don't like its history as a patriarchal institution that deliberately orchestrated the degradation of women for the last two thousand years. I don't like the hymns. Or reading in unison. I really don't get the Bible. The Bible worries me. When Dani sends me the scripture for that week's sermon I always think, *Oof. What the hell are we supposed to do with that turkey?*

I think this. *Every. Time.*

Yet Dani finds the quotidian poetry. From the elegance of the mustard seed, to the ache of Mary at the tomb, to the repetitive ramblings of Paul, Dani mines this ancient text for the human window—the soft spot in the words, or between the words. This is how she brings her congregation into the heart space.

Beginnings ❂ 13

She has a lot of ways of doing this. She often provides historical context. She occasionally sprinkles in an etymological reframe. She often considers the ways her congregation is hurting. She almost always includes examples from the daily monotony of the modern world. She is funny. She is not above a Salt-N-Pepa reference. She carefully confesses her own truths when she thinks it will serve. She makes space for individuality and resistance. In essence, she tells them a story. She uses scripture as the *basis* of the story, but in the end, she is really telling the congregation the story of *themselves*. The story of us all.

This is what a play should do.

But I can't just bring up the curtain and tell my audience to contemplate death. I can't just say, "Good evening everyone, please examine how to live." I have to tell them a story. That's what lured them to come to the play in the first place—they've been promised a story.

I have a lot of ways of doing this: I choose a world. I explore a subculture adjacent to our own—be it Amish culture or Civil War re-enactors or museum guards or a gynecological lab in the 1960s. I woo my audience to engage by presenting them with a world that appears different from their own. This requires research, and I often share that research with the audience. I carefully confess details of my own life when I think it will serve. I use humor. I am not above a fart joke. I cuss a little (actually a lot). I make us care about the characters and the situation they are navigating. This is how I bring the audience into the heart space.

Writing a play feels like being in a sanctuary. I feel in contact with a mysterious force. I remember clearly what it was like to discover this feeling. Writing my first play felt like what it must be like when a bird realizes those feathery things hanging on its side are for flying. Once I got a taste of that sky, I never looked back.

And then finally, deep into the play, there it is. The big truth. The spiritual truth. It's like all that character dialogue and action were really just hands rubbing together to make the thing we needed in the first place—the heat. The play isn't complete unless I've figured out what that truth is. And then I work on making the truth well-told. Like a sermon. You could say that at the heart of every play is a sermon.

Theater is always an invitation to heal. Which immediately begs the question—*Heal what?* I could (and probably will) spend my life contemplating that question.

What strikes me now, in the middle of my life (at least I hope), in the middle of my career (at least I hope), is the myth of Being Separate. Theater is a way to heal the idea that I'm over here and you are over there. Which is true, of course. I'm in my body having my life and my memories and worries and dreams and road rage and orgasms and farts and illnesses and panics and belly laughs. And someone else is having theirs. It's lonely. We bear these things alone most of the time.

But there's this thing around us. Like a fabric. Made of stars and water and tissue and minerals. Made of phosphorescent dust. Invisible and shimmering. Theater turns off the house lights and this ephemeral fabric suddenly shimmers around us, inside us, between us. This fabric catches the light from the stage and the magic ignites. We feel it. Our minds hook into the story, but another consciousness awakens. The Invisible Us starts looking around at the other Invisible Us-es and we glimpse it. The Myth of Being Separate is shattered.

If this isn't what religion is supposed to do, I don't know what is. Dani stands in front of her congregation every week (and every birth and every funeral and every wedding and every triple bypass surgery, every assisted living visit, every depressive episode) and urges them, assures them, begs them, to connect to their connectedness. To believe in it. To live into it. To share it with others.

Maybe that's why our collaboration works. She reads my play and engages with the practice of the long-form frame of the spiritual truth; I read her sermons and engage with the potent, immediate delivery of the spiritual truth. We each get to practice the end of the spectrum furthest from (but essential to) our own craft. And we make each other laugh.

That's how we got here. This book is another way to sister. And we get to do it together. That's the best part.

This entire book is a heart space.

WILDFLOWERS AND CUT GRASS

Dani

When I think of Jessie, I think of a field of wildflowers, an open field of wheat, golden and swaying in the breeze.

I'm like a lawn, cut grass and corners.

One time, when Jessie was getting ready to move, I took the train into New York so that I could clean out her junk drawers and organize them. When Jessie was going through a divorce, I completed all of her financial aid forms for graduate school. I relish the idea that someday I'll get to be her personal assistant and just organize the hell out of her schedule and closet.

Jessie, on the other hand, can look at a room and know exactly how to enhance it with furniture and color. She sends handwritten cards and letters to me, filled with details about her day and how she's feeling, with little people drawn in the margins. She can make conversation with anyone, and I don't mean small talk. Jessie has an incredible ability to draw out the story from another person.

If Jessie is a tape measure, I'm a ruler. She's a knit throw and I'm a sewn quilt. She's a tray of watercolors; I'm a packet of Sharpies.

You get it.

In the Bible, there are only a few stories explicitly about women, even though we know that women are always there, not just on the margins, but also in the center. Someone had to be making all those tunics and dyeing all that yarn and making all that food. Someone had to be doing all that labor. We have few stories where women are the center and even fewer examples of sisters, but one of them is the story of Mary and Martha. In the story, Jesus is visiting Mary and Martha in their home.

Martha is a doer. Mary is a listener. During Jesus's visit, Martha is all about getting things ready, preparing the meal, serving the guests. Mary, on the other hand, is sitting at Jesus's feet, soaking up his words, listening deeply. I can imagine her nodding her head, asking questions and opening herself up to his answers. Meanwhile, Martha is thrashing about in the background clanging pots and milking the goat; she's bringing plates of food out. Mary, imploring Martha to sit down and enjoy this moment and Martha, sighing loudly and cussing, "Can you guys just eat the g-d damn figs so I can serve the next course?"

I laugh every time I hear that story because Jessie is a Mary. She is intentional, she is devoted, she is open, she is grounded, she is always ready for a deep conversation, she is always poised to hear the truth in what others say.

I am a Martha. I like the feeling of usefulness. I like the labor of tasks that have beginnings and endings. I like listening to a story while I am chopping vegetables. I like anticipating needs and then meeting them.

Because both of our lives involve the daily practice of writing, I see these wildflowers and cut grass in our writing as well. So often, the ritual of sermon writing is an exercise in restraint. It takes focus. It takes creativity, too, of course, but it's always hemmed in by time and packaging. As the writer you walk down this corridor of a Biblical passage and you have to decide what door you'll be entering. In the story of Mary and Martha, for example, you could explore why Jesus was there at all. You could explore further what role Mary and Martha played in Jesus's ministry. You could explore (as I have in this essay) the idea that

Mary is a listener and Martha is a doer, or you could maybe even flip those assumptions on their head. You could explore a turn of phrase in what Jesus says, examining the original Greek, comparing translations. There are countless doors you could enter. It's a gift really, to have that many doors. In a ministry that spans decades, you often have to preach the same stories, over and over again, and each time, you try to find a different lens in the prism to hone your focus. In a first pass reading, I might find ten possible doors to open for a sermon; but a sermon can't address ten things. A sermon can, at best, address one thing, one topic and even then, that might be generous. After I research, when I get to the writing, I can open each door a little, I can acknowledge the possibilities a bit, but a good sermon won't open all the doors. A good sermon trusts that the Holy Spirit is pointing me in a direction for this week and believes that another truth will win the day next time.

When I first started preaching, finding the one thread to pull on in a scripture passage was hard. It felt constricting. It felt like I was doing a disservice to my congregation if I didn't tell them all the exegetical secrets of the passage. To cope with that, I developed a Martha style of writing—methodical, hemmed in, to the point. Efficient. There were years of sermon writing where I didn't type a single word before writing out a detailed, bullet-pointed outline. I had colored pens and legal pads for this purpose. It suited me well. It took years of methodical writing and colored-pen outlines before I started to feel my sermon writing come from a place that was heart-centered. I credit that shift to reading and talking about the plays that Jessie has written.

I notice that when Jessie writes, she first opens every door in the writing corridor. She mines every field. She turns over every stone, she goes down every tributary in pursuit of the story that is wanting to be told. Jessie can write with such depth and weave such a unique story because she opens the doors and explores what's behind them. When Jessie gets stuck in her writing, I know it's because all the doors are open. In the river of her play, she most often gets stuck because of all the tributaries she has gone down. She is aware of all the places she could go, the characters she needs to develop, the tender nuances of personality and plot that need to be flushed out.

When she can't find her way, I know my role. My role is to remind her of the river, remind her of the corridor, remind her of the core of her story and idea. What is the story she wants to tell? Sometimes that means asking her a question about the end goal; other times, it is recalling with her something she said four conversations ago about her protagonist. I try to stand in front of each door, close them and say, "not today" or "we can figure that out later." Sometimes, I tell her about what I would do in sermon writing (aka, one door only).

When I write a sermon, I have to trust that the Spirit will bring forth truth in spite of everything I *don't* say. When Jessie writes a play, she trusts that by opening every door, she'll be rewarded with a rich narrative that serves the reader and the story.

In the story of Mary and Martha, it kind of sounds like Mary is doing the wiser thing by choosing to sit and listen, to let Jesus's story unfold around her. Jesus even says so. But there are other stories in the Bible that would nod to those of us who are doers, those of us who are focused on outcome. The wounded man on the side of the road doesn't get help until the Good Samaritan—the person who can get shit done—comes along. Mary can sit at the feet of Jesus because Martha is creating the space for it to happen. And Martha can do her thing in the kitchen because Mary is attending to the important work of spending time with her friend.

Mary and Martha aren't opposites. Jessie and I aren't opposites. Sermon writing and playwriting aren't opposites. Though at first blush, one might think that. They are complementarians. I think God wants both—listeners and laborers. And what I've learned is that both are storytellers.

Both are necessary and both are useful in developing the other. Sometimes for the health of the grass, it needs to be cut. Sometimes, the wildflowers must have their way. Sometimes, it's their contrast that gives us the landscape.

TUESDAY MORNINGS

Dani

It's a Tuesday morning and my eyes fly open. Shit. It's 6:15. The sun has not even risen yet, but the house is already stirring. Alan is in the shower; my daughter Gracie is singing in her crib at the top of her lungs. I love that Jesus created her, my little spritely songbird, but Jesus did not make "Monkeys on the Bed" an appropriate song for 6 o'clock in the morning. And OHMYGOD, why am I so hot? It's like the heat of a thousand suns. Liam (my seven-year-old) found his way into our bed sometime in the night. His limbs are intertwined with mine, the blankets our cocoon. I am suffocating. I carefully unwrap Liam—no need to wake that dragon yet—and make my way to the bathroom to get ready. I'm mid-shower before my eleven-year-old yells through the door that he can't find his lunch and dad has gone and can I make him a lunch? Sigh. Yes. Lunch.

The morning continues like this: a series of small demands interspersed with cuddles and a blowout diaper and by the time I get to work it's like I've run some kind of marathon—or at least it would be if I was at all interested in being a runner. Which I'm not. I can already feel what the day is going to be like, the morning a harbinger of things to come. The days are just like this, chaotic and harried, full of blessing but also full of little crises and tasks that need attending and that's not just because I have children, it is also the pace of my life as a pastor.

The first memory I have of church is sitting under the desk in my Grampy's office. I am two and I have curled up at his feet with a pad of pink paper used for jotting down phone messages. I have a pen and am making markings on the paper. Every few moments he slips me another page and on it he has drawn a picture of two cats sitting on a picket fence looking at the moon. At the base of the fence is a little mouse. In retrospect, I am sure that the secretary and other pastors knew I was there under the desk, but at the time, I felt hidden, a co-conspirator with my grandfather. I remember feeling safe and valued. I remember knowing that he was glad that I was there.

Even now, when I try to conjure up an image of what it means to be in the presence of God, or what God might look like, this is the image that comes to mind. Sitting at the feet of a loving presence. I cannot see everything from where I am sitting, but I can feel that I am wanted and known. I can feel that I am safe. Now, as a minister almost 40 years later, that imagery is close to what I envision my role as pastor to be. To help people feel safe. Valued. Important. Understood. Or at least to hear from me that God sees them as important. God understands them. God wants them to be safe. God values them.

On my favorite days in ministry, I feel the joy of that opportunity, the privilege of it. I get to rejoice in the gifts of others, celebrate their uniqueness, and push them towards using those gifts for God's purposes. On my favorite days in ministry, *I* feel useful and valued and understood. I feel important. Not self-important. I feel important in the way that my contribution matters.

The reality is that most days in ministry, I try to be and do those things, in between writing a bulletin, or cleaning out a refrigerator so I can find where that smell is coming from, or crawling in a closet because I'm sure there is a Jesus puppet somewhere in there. And always in the background, the ever-present specter of the sermon—the beat of the Sunday drum thrumming ever closer as the week goes on.

I love my calling, but let's stop right now and get one thing straight: There are some weeks where I welcome writing a sermon about as much as I welcome a family of lice taking up residence in my hair.

I just don't want to. Sometimes, I don't want to because the week has been oppressively busy, my office door and my inbox inundated with requests ranging from minutiae to existential questions. Or maybe it's just busy because one of my kids has strep throat and my cat won't stop throwing up and sitting down at the computer is just one thing that has to wait.

Other times, I don't want to write a sermon because of the world. Another school shooting. Another act of violence rooted in racism or homophobia. Another hurricane hit, another humanitarian disaster in the news. The compassion fatigue hits hard and strong and I just don't want to weave the words together, I don't want to knit the delicate balance between lament and hope.

And still other times, and maybe this is most weeks, I am mad or flummoxed or bereft or bored at what's on the page, the words in the Biblical passage. It's not always easy to find meaning and purpose in this web of stories that is often patriarchal and difficult to understand. I read the passage and I think, "does it *really* have to say that?" The imperfect words of imperfect people, attempting to describe what we hope for in a perfect God.

Someone annoyingly once said, "Sunday comes every week." Eye roll. I know. Don't you see that's why I'm tired? Sunday comes every week and God's mercy is new every morning. Or something.

I sit down at the computer. I type the words, "I don't know what you want me to say." It helps to put that on the page. Each keystroke a proverbial stomp of the foot, a whine to God. But it helps. Something about it loosens whatever is causing the tightness in my chest. The first words of the sermon usually come to me in this way—when I start by saying the first thing in my brain, the thing that needs to be said before the deeper thing can be said.

It's unbecoming, as a pastor, to have an internal temper tantrum about God's word, but I also sense that this is one of the many ways that the body of Christ is connected—through our collective tantrum at God's word (or the people's words about God). We grunt and roll our eyes and stumble around and shrug our shoulders and think it has nothing to do with right now because we are tired and overwhelmed and anxious and don't want these complex emotions to be oversimplified. The truth is, what I bring to preaching is often connected to my congregation's collective consciousness. If I feel frustrated or uncertain or confused—I am often not far off from what the Spirit is sharing with me about where my people are.

"Who am I that I should go to Pharaoh and deliver the people out of Egypt?" says Moses.

"Who am I that I should deliver this message, me who is so young?" says Jeremiah, the prophet.

"Who am I that I should be the one to deliver a message that I *really* don't want to say?" says Jonah.

Time and time again in scripture, people are resistant to preach and hear the message and direction of God. Why should it be any different now? Why should my resistance not be yet another place God's voice is made manifest?

Because time and time again, the word *does* get preached, most often because God insists. God compels. God requires that I take whatever it is I bring to the week and put it on the page, bring it to the pulpit. God insists that whatever lines I have drawn between the sacred and profane be blurred and even erased, in favor of something messier but truer. Because a real sermon—born out of the real things, the snotty noses, the laughing children, the heartbreaking death, the troubling budget, the infuriating injustice—is a holy sermon that brings me far closer to God's story than any glossed and gussied up version of truth that I could come up with without the influence of actual life.

"I don't know what you want me to say," I type, "but I guess I'll try and freaking say it."

And the page breaks open. The words come. The Spirit works through me and in spite of me and with me.

And then we begin again, but this time, it's Wednesday.

WHEN WE GET STUCK

Jessie

I think about the dark. People sitting in the dark. The way hearts flower open like nightshades in the dark. I imagine I'm sitting in the dark with them. Waiting. Watching the small stage in front of us. But I'm also on the stage—connected to what is on the stage. I wait until I sense something true. 'Til something true speaks from the dark. Then I let the character begin right there.

Or sometimes I go for a walk. Or a yoga class.

Sometimes I buy something. Like a fancy candle. Or a lipstick. Or that birthday gift. These retail solutions are interesting, almost like a vote of confidence in my ability to solve this problem. The part of me that feels like an Imposter Writer might say, "You can't buy something! You're an artist and you're poor and all of this is precariously pinned and may fall apart at any moment! Just stay home and miserably plug away!" Whereas the successful, Confident Writer in me is like, "You've got this. Take a break. Go enjoy the world. You'll figure this one out and get another one. And then another one." It works.

You know what also works? Sending Dani the entire piece of crap draft and saying, "Please hellllllllppppp." She's *really good* at giving notes and brainstorming ideas. That's what I do when I get stuck.

It strikes me now that Dani is really the only person I have ever talked to when I'm stuck.

This started young.

Dani was the only person I told in exacting and agonizing detail how humiliated I was by a boy's rejection. Dani was the only person I talked to about my money worries. Or being burned out and exhausted. Out in the world of Waynesboro I felt the need to maintain a tough poise. Maybe that was being a teacher's kid. Or a coach's athletic kid. Dani was the only person I showed my full self.

When Dani gets stuck, it's usually because she's tired. Her stores are empty. From nurturing everyone around her.

Tending to every frustrated disappointment (including mine), every tearful fear (even mine), even every ignorant bliss (including mine). So it's about filling her stores. Or at least holding her for a while, letting her rest. Making her laugh.

This started young.

Once I put a bloody Always pad under Dani's pillow.

Well, it wasn't *bloody*; it was decorated to *look* bloody. Shocking red nail polish streaked across the pristine pad. I had also drawn a Dracula face with fangs, dripping with nail polish blood. Bloody red letters scrawled, "Dani, I vant to suck your blood!"

This was the eighties.

I had been intensely, earnestly praying for my period to arrive (yup, I prayed about it). I was super keen to get this Womanhood thing going. I had written to the Always feminine products company to send me the Always Preteen Package (complete with illustrated explanation pamphlet and sample products). And it was from said Always Preteen Package that I procured the materials for my Dracula bloody pad prank. When Dani's scream lanced the house, I knew she'd found it.

On another occasion I stood on our parents' bed with no pants above a discouraged Dani and performed James Taylor's "You've Got a Friend" while shaking the ample cellulite I had already acquired by age sixteen.

It's not like the bloody pad or James Taylor cellulite concert are the perfect solution for getting Dani unstuck in her sermon writing *every time*. But this style of tactic is definitely still in my arsenal. The way to help Dani get unstuck in her sermon writing is to give her a break. To shift her energy. To brainstorm solutions.

Sometimes when she's stuck, I ask her if there's something in the sermon she wants to say but feels she cannot.

Because Dani's congregation is politically diverse—a rare strength that Dani wants to protect—the events of the world and her own feelings about it do not necessarily make space for the spectrum of belief in her pews. So she has to contort around that, curb her words, and that often costs her. I never have any idea how Dani should navigate something like that. But if we can identify that struggle and she can talk it out, identify what the text calls up for her and suss out how to make room for that truth too, the right path presents itself and she can open up. The sermon can flow.

If not, there's always James Taylor.

CHURCH MAKES ME CRY

Jessie

Church makes me cry.

I have no idea why. It bewilders me. Every time. Because in truth, there is not much I enjoy about church. Not even the hymns. Especially not the hymns. They're the opposite of catchy and always written in a key that's too high. People don't really sing along, they sort of squeak.

But sure enough, I cry.

I recently saw a play at a very old theater in Paris. We ran late, rushed to our velvet seats in the back of the orchestra. The audience hummed with their digesting dinners. An actor came out from behind the curtain and began addressing the audience. I smiled. I love direct address, when the playwright has the character/actor directly speak to the audience before them. "Breaking the fourth wall" is what it's called—the wall that "separates" the audience from the action on the stage. Direct address removes that fourth wall, allows the character/actor to acknowledge that they know the audience is there while also allowing the audience to know that in fact this is playing out in front of them for their benefit. But it was when the ensemble began streaming in through the aisle up the left side of the house that I began to cry. And then openly weep. Twenty actors poured onto the stage. The play began with a Christmas party. They lit candles and shook champagne bottles, spraying huge diaphanous arcs across the stage, laughing, raucous, joyful. I thought, clear as a bell, "What a privilege it is to have them play in front of us." Right there. We can touch their skirt. We can see the dirty smudge on their boot. We can see what their belly does when they breathe. The way they favor their left leg a little when they rise out of the chair. These are things you can *choose* to show on camera. But in the delicious chaos of a huge ensemble party scene, you can see how this character exhales after her husband laughs too loud, how the women smile knowingly about an inside joke, how someone upstage is picking lint off their sleeve.

I cried in that moment because I miss theater. I worry about theater. I don't want it to disappear. I love it and I believe in it, and it's endangered.

Much of the same could be said for church. But do I miss church? Did I once "have church" and now I don't? And my body remembers even if my mind doesn't? Like church is something that used to be inside me and is now gone.

In French, the nature of the verb *manquer*—*to miss*—requires placing the object you are missing in front of the verb and yourself. So if I miss you, it's *Tu me manques*. You are missing from me. If I miss church, *L'eglise me manque*. You encounter the thing you miss before you realize the missing. *Church is missing from me.*

Christmas Eve was by far the best service at our childhood church. The sanctuary had pale green walls and high white windows. The organ would vibrate in my stomach and the poinsettias were blood red below the gold cross on the white marble altar. My favorite part of the service was when we would light candles and sing Silent Night. We would each hold a small white candle with its paper circle to catch the wax. The ushers would light the flame at the end of each aisle, and each person would pass the flame to the candle next to them until the entire sanctuary was glowing. During the final refrain of "Silent Night" the entire congregation would lift their candle in the air. It was hushed and holy.

I don't know when I lost church. Or why.

I watched my mom lose something of church during our childhood. Her father was a UCC minister, just like Dani. His gentle way of holding church was part of our childhood atmosphere. I remember in seventh grade we were learning how to debate, and we were assigned a group and given a topic to debate with another group. My group was given Evolution vs. Creationism, and I was randomly assigned to the Creationism group. I asked my grandfather how he held science next to his religious beliefs, because I knew he loved science. I remember my grandfather pointing out astronomy and constellations when I was little when he ran a Christian education camp in central Pennsylvania. He told me that he believed all of science only revealed the intelligence and sensitivity of God. For him there was absolutely no conflict between the two.

Grampy served as the minister of pastoral care at our childhood church. As he declined in age and health, they basically forced him to retire. He never said a nay word about the church or any of the people involved in this, but I remember my mom crying with rage. She continued to attend that church, but the shadow of the church's pettiness hung over her from then on.

Not long after, it was time for me to be confirmed and become a member of the church. I declined. When it was time to stand in front of the congregation and testify that this is what I believe, I told my parents I didn't want to. It would be a lie. I'm not sure if this was consciously connected to the souring of Grampy's relationship with the church and my mother's grief on his behalf, but it must have been difficult for both my grandparents and my mother to watch. The church and its progressive path to faith had been the center of their lives. It must have saddened them to see me turn away. But they respected my decision and let it stand as that—my decision.

And yet, still today, church makes me cry.

I like going to Dani's church because there is a genuine culture of kindness. But mostly because I love seeing her do what she does. Though it's also weird. I've heard that for the loved ones of an artist, it can be disconcerting to see their art, whether they've written something or they are performing in it. I think it's because when you love someone, part of that love is knowing them. But seeing their art inevitably means encountering the side of them that you don't know, that in fact belongs to the world, not to you.

This is also true for clergy. When Dani is in the pulpit I'm confronted with a disconnect between the sister I talk to every day and the person speaking. Chances are I even proofread the sermon she's delivering. But I still feel disoriented. I'm seeing her *in role*. It's disconcerting to see the congregation think she belongs to them. I sit in my pew and think, "Au contraire, mes amies. I know the Real Dani."

But the truth is, they know a Dani I will never know: They know Dani the spiritual mother. Dani the extension of a benevolent God. Dani the bearer of the host. The holder of the sacred cup. Dani the proxy of forgiveness and peace. She sits next to their hospital bed, she presides over their wedding, their funeral, their marriage troubles, their loneliness, their joys and their concerns.

She does all this for me too. But with a lot more cuss words.

And yet...

Sometimes I'll be walking down the street, or in the middle of a meeting, and I'll suddenly remember that Dani believes in Jesus Christ.

It'll hit me, just like that.

I walk around all day believing in *something*. It has something to do with humanity and goodness, sprinkled with a little nature woo-woo and intelligent design. I call myself an Agnostic. But really I'm just wishy-washy.

Dani?—*actually believes*.

Not to say what she believes is *simple*. Not at all. Her beliefs are hard-earned and well-seasoned with nuance and humility and the rigor of disciplined study. She did the time. She got the degree. And she really lives in the world; she's not naive. In fact, Dani knows more about most things than anyone I know. Because she has been alongside hundreds of other humans in all of their life events, Dani is carrying an encyclopedia of human experience. It's staggering. From what happens in hospice, to the nitty gritty of a medical procedure, to insurance policies and estate management, to woodwork and teachers unions and retirement services and childcare subsidies and public funding for anything and everything. I hear about her moments with parishioners every single day (never their names because she is a beast for confidentiality). But still—sometimes I will be in the middle of an errand or quotidian task, and I'll remember: Dani *believes*.

I admire that. I would envy it except I see what it costs. The kind of faith Dani has demands action. It requires constant discomfort and engagement. It exacts heartache. And to be the apex of that belief for a large community of people requires constant restraint. And loneliness. And exhaustion.

But truly, I would like to believe.

Maybe when I cry in church, I'm crying for my wishy-washy Agnosticism.

Maybe I'm crying for my grandfather's dignity. And my mother's painful childhood as a Preacher's Kid.

Maybe I'm crying for the futility that threatens Dani's faith as she confronts our broken country.

Maybe I'm crying because when it comes to religion, the whole world is truly broken.

Maybe I'm crying because somewhere in the origins of my consciousness, in the dawn moments of my beginning, I felt connected to something, something that determined who I am and why I am, and I don't feel connected to it anymore. Not unless I'm sitting in seats surrounded by other people. Listening to a voice in the dark. With words that someone sat alone and wrote. Imagining their way to the future ear of an aching heart.

Maybe I'm crying because church and theater are supposed to make us cry. To make us feel. To connect us to the heart. Our own and everyone else's. Whether the key is too high or the words aren't my own or in an unintelligible foreign language, maybe I'm crying because the words don't actually matter. It's the invisible thing inside them, below them, that I'm hearing. My heart speaks that language. And responds with its own voice.

FUNERALS AND GOODBYES

Dani

You wouldn't think cars have to do with loss, but they do. I'm sitting in my car, second in line in the funeral procession. I've just said the words of commendation at the end of the service in the sanctuary, the words I speak at every funeral, "Into your hands, O merciful Savior, we commend your servant. Acknowledge, we humbly pray, a sheep of your own fold, a lamb of your own flock, a child of your own redeeming. Receive them into the blessed rest of everlasting peace and into the company of the saints in light." Then we piled into cars to go to the cemetery.

A funeral procession is supposed to have the right of way but whether or not that will happen is always a question mark. Sometimes, the drivers are impatient. Sometimes they don't stop. Sometimes they stop but you can see the drivers roll their head back in their seat or rub their faces in frustration. When I see their inconvenienced huffing, a flare of anger shoots through me because there are precious few things that we center around as a culture anymore, precious few things we universally agree on, and it feels like giving space for grief should be one of them.

During the funeral, prior to the processional, I have tried to honor the truth of the deceased with kindness by illuminating what we want to remember, without hiding the things that were difficult. In my reflections about the deceased, I might recall the way their mom, who worked in an enamel tooth factory, would bring home tiny factory tooth rejects and paint little faces on them, to the delight of her children. I might share the way their grandpa had a newspaper route, well into his nineties. I might recall for them the memories of their loved one saying gentle words before walking down the aisle, or the way they belly laughed on road trips.

But we are never just one person and so sometimes it means I am acknowledging with the family that alcohol played too big a role in their loved one's coping strategies. Or a quiet acknowledgement that these sisters never found their way back after a falling out. Or a nod to the complicated family dynamics after a divorce. For whatever the perceived purpose of the funeral—closure, ritual, finality—in truth, it is most especially the time when we leave space. Space for grief and meaning making. Space for the holy.

We get in our cars and let them carry our grief because once the spell is broken, once the space for the holy has ended, the "Life After" begins.

You wouldn't think that cars have to do with loss, but they do.

The sistering between Jessie and me really hit its stride thanks to a car. My whole life I crawled into bed with her, or played ponies with her, or traded back rubs, but something shifted when our sistering got the wings of a driver's license. Jessie got her driver's license at sixteen, when I was thirteen. It was the *perfect* age difference. She was old enough to drive, and I was old enough that my parents let me go anywhere with her. That meant we drove around. A lot. We careened around the back roads of our Pennsylvania town, taking the "long way" home so we could talk and listen to music. We'd take on personas in our singing, or dance in ways to make the other laugh. At first it was all in a brown station wagon (The Beast), then it was in a car that smelled like cat pee (The Cat Car), then it was in a teal Jetta (Heather). It didn't matter. We had the open road and that's where our relationship began to exist outside of our home.

When I was a freshman in high school, Jessie was a senior. At that point, we'd been driving around for two years and so our secret society was rock solid. Generally speaking, Jessie and I did not do any of the typical teenage rebellion tropes. We didn't drink, we didn't smoke pot, we didn't lie to our parents (to be fair, that was less about who we were and more about who they were). But we weren't above a little truancy. On one such day, we plotted and planned to skip out during the two-hour period midday when we both had lunch and band. We walked out to the car, parked in the back of the high school, like we had every right to be doing it. As we were making our way to the car, the truancy officer came rolling by and asked where we were going. Without missing a beat, Jessie pipes in, "Oh my sister got her period—we're going out to the car to get tampons."

I quickly wrapped my hands around my abdomen and gave my best "pained cramping" look.

"Oh okay. Just make sure to get back quickly."

They were embarrassed and drove away. We were triumphant.

With a whoop and holler, we got in our car and crossed state lines to our favorite lunch destination for bread bowls filled with creamy soup. Who was going to stop us? We were sisters—and the strength of that was intoxicating.

By the time Jessie was leaving for college, my confidence in the world was firmly wrapped up in having her close. I did not realize how much I felt the ghost warmth of her beside me in my classes, in my conversations, in the lunchroom. I didn't understand the security I intuited from knowing that I could find her in the hallway and she would swoop me away for reassurance and laughter. Now she was leaving, and not just down the road. She was going really far away—to Boston. I was torn. I knew she needed that freedom, she needed to spread out and grow and be away from Waynesboro, but it was hard not to equate that with her wanting to be away from me. She seemed so ready for it, and I was most certainly not.

The night before she left, we had plans.

In our sweatpants and messy buns, we drove down to Hagerstown—a quick twenty-minute drive—blasting Beastie Boys and Lauryn Hill, and we hit up our favorite donut shop, open only late at night. We grabbed our chocolate-covered cream-filled donuts and drove around. The kind of long, meandering drive where we rolled the windows down, sang out loud, and cruised on country roads.

But it was past midnight and Jessie was leaving early in the morning and so our goodbye processional was coming to a close. The processional that included the rituals of our sisterhood (food, music, laughter) was nearing its end and the goodbye was oppressively close. Maybe that's why it was on the way back into town, past the blinking lights that told us we were getting close that we spotted it—one of those green road signs that said, "WAYNESBORO."

"We need that sign."

"You think we can?"

"Of course we can."

"Flip this bitch!" (our charming expression for a U-turn), "We'll get it."

It was the perfect capstone to our final hurrah. And like the truancy officer and the tampons, we approached that sign with unreasonable confidence. We could totally get that sign down. It's the middle of the night, on a deserted country road. No one will catch us and Jessie will have a souvenir. What could possibly go wrong?

The sign was posted along the side of the road where there was a drainage ditch running alongside it. To access the sign, which was a good eight feet off the road, there was no way to be stealthy. I had to climb on her shoulders, along the side of the road, and try to pry the screws loose. A nice little misdemeanor to crown the night. We tried. For an hour.

Those suckers are on there tight. It's like they knew some trashy teenagers would try to steal it and make it their own.

We didn't want to break the law, what we wanted was something to mark the occasion. I wanted the pause of recognition that something magical had happened over the last sixteen years—and anything that came before it and after it would be marked by this friendship, this sisterhood. When the goodbye processional ended, we'd have something that bound us to it.

It felt unreasonable that the sign was on so tight when we wanted it—needed it. It felt like an affront to my grief that this night couldn't be enshrined in a green street sign hanging in her dorm room. Without a reminder of me hanging in her dorm room, would I cease to exist? If the truth of it wasn't there with her, would all that was left be my mythologizing of our relationship? Was it as great as I remembered if she wasn't physically there with me anymore? That damn sign would not budge. We drove home. The spell broken. She left the next day. Another kind of "Life After" beginning.

It was natural and good that she left, but it didn't feel natural and good that the leaving didn't include me. It felt unfair that she could build what she wanted while I had to return to what we had together and find my way in it without her. In her departure, it felt like I was left to live where *we* lived, drive where *we* drove, eat where *we* ate. All without the "we."

Death and departure are not the same of course, but they are echoes of one another, both grounded by grief. These goodbyes remind us that there are places our loved ones go, where we cannot follow. There are experiences our loved ones have that we cannot go through with them.

No matter the bonds we have formed, there are some roads that must be traveled alone.

PART TWO

bodies

WHEN I DIDN'T ANSWER

Jessie

Moments after my sister was raped, she called and I didn't answer.

That sentence just sat by itself on the page for about fifteen minutes, the cursor blinking blankly, waiting. Blink. Blink. The cursor is like a thin bar in a line-high jail. The line disappears, suddenly opening a brief, white question—the space where I can continue, where I must continue. Then when I don't, the line reappears as if to say, "Still waiting."

Blink. Blink.

I was asleep. That's the simple answer. But oh, how I have worried—was I asleep? What if I actually rolled over and saw the call come in and simply rolled back over? What if I heard the ring and didn't even roll over? My rational brain knows I would never have done that. If Dani called in the middle of the night, I would know something was wrong. What if I saw the call and knew something was wrong and *did not want to know what*? I don't know. I just know that moments after my sister was raped, she called and I didn't answer.

I did answer the next morning. Or maybe I called her when I saw the missed call? I don't remember how we got on the phone. I remember talking in the living room of my college apartment—the second floor of an old house in Allston, Massachusetts. Made of dark wood, thick bushes huddled against the house on the front lawn, skunks huddled inside the bushes. Every night that I walked home from theater rehearsal, a long, physical ordeal that followed each day's theater classes (also long, physical ordeals), I would inevitably see that familiar, dreaded waddle of a white stripe against a furry black mass. That would have been the case on this particular night. I usually got home around 11:30. I would have eaten a bowl of cereal and crashed to bed, exhausted.

I shared that apartment with two other women—Liza, an actress in my program, and Lynn, a visual artist. I was hardly ever home; conservatory training days were long and arduous. Sometimes in the living room would be evidence of whatever exhibition Lynn was working on—I remember there was a string of beads that stretched from the dark wood floor to the ceiling. The beads were arranged in a pattern—twenty-eight taupe-colored beads, then six crimson-colored beads, then another twenty-eight taupe, then six crimson. The final exhibit was called "The Menstrual Hut." Dozens of string beads rose out of a dirt floor, reflecting the cycles of women's red insides rising up in synchrony.

After I hung up with Dani, Liza was in the kitchen. I said, "Dani was raped last night." Then I went to class.

Blink. Blink.

In many ways my years at Boston University were my happiest yet. I'd always been certain I would make a life in the theater. Which means I'd always been certain I would leave my small town. Dani sat on the bed while I packed. She was bereft. I was on the edge of being free. I felt guilty, but some deep, unconscious instinct coiled that guilt into a tight fist inside me that told me, "Go."

Boston University was an avalanche of new experiences—each day surrounded by other young theater artists hungry to immerse into our craft, to push our bodies, our voices, our hearts, to their outer limits. We stretched and howled and improvised and studied and scarfed food while we memorized our text. Over and over, every single day, we stood in the front of the room and exposed something of our interiority—tears and pain and memory stored inside our bodies, the narrative of our family of origin, the various wounds and ticks of our personalities. All this had to be unearthed, harnessed; this is how you train your instrument.

All my classmates knew Dani. She'd been to visit, of course. She'd tolerated my college boyfriend and we'd gone shopping at Copley Square, seen a movie with popcorn, Milk Duds and Coke. (Which doesn't look right on the page, because when discussing said movie plans it was always "PopcornMilkDudsandCoke.") Then we'd crawled into my bed together and fallen asleep talking.

But really my classmates all knew Dani because I'd been making theater about her since I'd arrived at Boston University's BFA program four years earlier.

Our first assignment was to dramatize a dream. My group re-enacted a nightmare that plagued me for many weeks when we first moved into the big house on Seventh Street, when I was five and Dani was two-and-a-half: A woman in a billowing white nightgown was floating down the hall. Her nightgown reflected on the gleaming dark wood floor below her. It was a thunderous night and the hall was lined with room-high windows. White curtains billowed with every flash of lightning. I knew I had to get Dani away from the woman. I was afraid that if she found us, she would beat Dani, even though I knew I was the bad one. In one version of the dream, I was able to get us out of the house and we ran through the dark rain to the John Wallace diner on Main Street where we called for help from a payphone. My mother and I would go to the John Wallace for hot chocolate after my piano lessons. The banquettes were covered in orange, plastic seat covering. The walls glowed with a warm, wine color. In my dream, Dani and I shivered outside the John Wallace in a phone booth trying to call for help. Dani was wet and shivering, and I was trying to cover her with wet, white towels. I had to raise up on my tiptoes to push the metallic buttons. I don't know who I thought I was calling.

Years later, as this dream was dramatized in my freshman theater class, Acting and the Ensemble, a small brown-haired girl named Rihanna played Dani. Her jaw and her body shivered while a tall girl named Andrea coldly circled in a flowing white sheet. The ensemble repeated "Dani Dani Dani" like an incantation. Like a prayer.

Blink. Blink.

I met her rapist the weekend before it happened.

I was home from Boston and my parents and I traveled together down to DC to visit her campus. I had been hearing about him. Dani told me about the complicated nuance of their bourgeoning friendship. I didn't like the way he talked about her body. He told Dani he always recognized her across the campus because of the way her ass moved from side to side. I got that that was sexy. That Dani found him sexy. But I also knew he had a darkness.

He'd earned a scholarship to American University for serving as a war correspondent during the ethnic cleansing in the former Yugoslavia in the 1990s. He was exotic, forged by a burned-out childhood in his war-torn country. Brilliant, worldly, damaged, and terribly charismatic, he was just a freshman, like Dani, but he was already a man.

So I hated his guts.

And then suddenly he was in front of us. We were about to go out to dinner and my parents had waited in the car while Dani and I retrieved something from her room. We crossed the quad outside the dorm they shared and there he was. His eyes were like bruises. Looking at him, the hunch of his shoulders, I didn't feel hate at all. I felt sad. Later at the restaurant, Dani and I went to the bathroom together and I said, "Be careful. You can't save him."

Blink. Blink.

Dani had always been beautiful, even in childhood photos (when no one has a right to be beautiful). She had big, blue eyes and a mischievous, cherry mouth. Her creamy, round face was framed in shiny, brown curls. Little, shapely legs stuck out of her roly-poly belly. She was an absolute honey bunny. Just describing her returns me to an overwhelming urge to kiss her. (Which I did. A lot. There is photographic evidence of this.)

In high school this meant she was a hottie. But Dani was also genuinely open, kind, even innocent. So her beauty was seasoned with something almost like naiveté. It was utterly endearing, if not downright remarkable. But it also made her vulnerable.

She told me that Todd Ramsey had been saying sexually explicit things to her in math class. I was a senior at Waynesboro Senior High and she was a freshman. At first she tried to laugh off his aggressive comments, but he persisted.

Todd Ramsey also had a beauty—the kind born of small-town privilege, the ease of being a decent sized fish in an anemic, small pond. His parents had money, which meant he could afford his signature Soccer Guy look—Tommy Hilfiger jeans and a colored polo shirt. Puma sneakers. He wasn't a bad kid. His freckled face and shaggy brown hair were as easy as his smug laugh.

I found him alone in the hallway near the front office. Shiny, beige floor tiles perpendicular to shiny, beige walls. I approached calmly and kept approaching until his back was against the wall. His freckled face, three or four inches below mine, drained of color. It was like we were instantly encased in an invisible, small room. My voice was very quiet. I had a sense that all of my being, still barely even known to me at seventeen, funneled wholly into my words.

"The way you talk to my sister makes her uncomfortable." Todd Ramsey swallowed. A little air escaped from his nose. "Do you know what I'm talking about?"

He nodded.

I waited a beat, and then said very quietly, very clearly, "That's going to stop now. Or next time I will have an administrator with me. Do you understand?"

He nodded again. His eyes never left mine.

As I walked away from Todd Ramsey, I discovered something I had never felt before—my power. It was easy to be powerful for Dani. She deserved it. She was my job.

I didn't understand that right away. It took about a week after my mother came home from the hospital with baby Dani before I asked, exasperated, "Where is her mommy?" My mother promptly delivered the bad news that *she* was her mommy.

But I figured out pretty early that Dani was my job. And for the most part I liked it. What better companion for rummaging through the couch cushions for small change so we could walk down the alley to the High's convenience store and buy a candy bar? Dani was a great second banana. There was never a moment that I realized we were a cult of two. We just were. Discovering a new layer of my identity by defending Dani from Todd Ramsey was just part of the natural process by which my identity had always been discovered. And by high school I had started to understand that boys were something we had to protect ourselves from.

It would prove more gnarly to translate that to men.

Mr. M was the father of my first serious boyfriend. I'd met Austin at a dinner theater considered a "sister" to the one I'd been working in for several years. Austin went to a magnet high school for the performing arts in Frederick, Maryland. Our parents became friends. So that my boyfriend and I could spend time together on the weekends, our parents made an arrangement that I would stay at his house. They had a guest room. Our contract was that Austin and I would always end up in separate rooms.

On one such occasion, I awoke in the middle of the night to find Mr. M standing in the doorway, watching me sleep. I remember even in my hazy half-awake state I felt . . . *exposed*. I didn't have a shirt on?—or maybe just a really thin tank top or something—and I rolled over to cover my chest. I told myself that he was probably just making sure that my boyfriend had gone to the other room, as per our arrangement. But Mr. M had long been a topic of discussion between Dani and me. You see, I'd be tracking how often he touched me. He had never specifically touched me *sexually*. I just always felt like he was *feeling* me.

Dani was one of the only people I talked to about this. She and I had both been indoctrinated to consider the feelings of others before our own, particularly those of men. I knew Mr. M cared about me and I believed it was simply that he had attached daughter-like affection for me and he did not realize that his touching bothered me. I worried it was my own neuroticism and insecurity that experienced Mr. M as oppressive. As a means of both obsession and distraction, I created experiments.

One was called The Hug Experiment. The premise was simple—when Mr. M approached for a hug, I would go "under" in the hug, forcing him to go "over." I was testing to see if in fact Mr. M always found a way to end with both hands on my waist. If I went "under" for the hug, he would naturally have to go "over," and that was not the natural direction of my waist. Dani watched from the side as I conducted my experiment. Somehow his hands still ended up on my waist. This went on long after Austin and I had broken up. We remained friends with the M family and even as I found ways to avoid him, Dani and I kept an open knowing between us about it.

It would not be until my freshman year of college, through the body work and personal excavation that theater training demands, that I would realize with visceral certainty that Mr. M had *known* that I didn't like the way he touched me, and he'd done it anyway.

Dani was now a sophomore in high school, and while home for the Christmas break I had been flooded with the remorse that I had inadvertently modeled to Dani that we should protect the feelings of men. That we had to put up with a certain amount of sexual attention. That it was our job to absorb the discomfort and make it okay. I remember telling her that I was going to confront Mr. M. I was conscious of trying to put us on the right path, to officially change our policy in this area. I felt responsible for both of us.

I am fully aware of the unabashed narcissism festooning this narrative. Like a gaudy ribbon garlanding around the authentic strength of my sister's individuality, her sovereignty. It curdles as soon as it goes on the page, this pathetic self-importance that told me I was Dani's protector. It's cliché. It's gross. It's demeaning. But I really believed it. I probably still do.

I did confront Mr. M. A week later Mrs. M sent a box to my mother with all the photos of our family in their house. We never saw them again.

But I had shown Dani the error of my ways. I'd righted the wrong. The record was amended. Nonetheless...

Moments after my sister was raped, she called and I didn't answer.

Over the course of the week that followed the rape, Dani and I talked every day, often multiple times per day. I followed her lead: Sometimes we were sarcastic about the rape; dry, dark. Some days we were crying, overwhelmed with grief. Some days we didn't talk about it at all, we acted like everything was the way it had been before. And as long as we talked every day, as long as we were still Jessie and Dani, it was.

Until a week later.

My parents called. They had heard from Dani's friend Kelly, who felt Dani was considering a suicide attempt. She was lining people up to cover her tasks at church, she told Kelly where she kept her keys, her wallet. She had been cutting her arms, trying to see something real on the outside for the invisible thing that consumed her inside. My parents called on their way to the hospital. Dani had agreed to be admitted.

This was the moment. My failure could not be denied. Could not be kept back. Dani had suffered an unimaginable act of violence, betrayal, desecration, injustice, abuse. She had survived it. She had reached for her phone and she had called me. If ever she needed a big sister it was right then—*right then*—and she did not have one. She had an aspiring thespian who was rehearsing fucking Pirandello. She had a Bostonite dodging skunks and wolfing cereal. She had a deep sleeper—or a lazy phone-call receiver—or a selfish self-absorbed narcissist—whatever. But she did not have what she needed.

Her sister.

Blink. Blink.

She did everything right. She kept her clothes. She called the DC rape hotline. She woke a friend and they went to the emergency room. She was nineteen and therefore an adult, and if she didn't feel like one before, she sure as shit became one right then.

She declined the rape kit because she knew they would find evidence of rape and she was not prepared, reeling in trauma and about to begin a long and painful battle with PTSD, to send her attacker back to his war-torn country still recovering from genocide. And maybe also because she still believed it was her job to absorb it and make it okay. I don't know because I was not right by her side hashing it out with her. I would try to do that in the coming months, years. But in that overwhelming moment of pain and terror and shame, Dani had to hash it out alone. And you know what?

She did.

UNANSWERED CALLS

~ ❀ ~

Dani

I've often wondered why the sister-osmosis connection didn't work that night. Innumerable times in our lives, Jessie has called me just as I was picking up the phone to call her. Still other times, I have found myself inexplicably crying only to find out later that as I was crying, she was too. The first time I recall the unspoken language between us was in the Friendly's restaurant in the Hagerstown Mall. Jessie got the hot dog. I got the grilled cheese. The waiter set our food down. There was a pause and without saying a word, we switched plates and each enjoyed the meal the other had ordered. Part of what makes up our special sister sauce is the communication that happens when there aren't words.

But not that night, and I can't wrap my head around why. Why, despite the most profound of connections between us, didn't she sense the danger I was in? Why didn't she experience a crack in her own heart as mine was breaking? Why didn't she just know to pick up the phone?

It was one o'clock in the morning. I was in a ball under the covers in my dorm room bed. I'd pressed my back against the corner of the wall, making myself as small as possible. My eyes swollen from crying and a dull ache radiating between my legs, the phone crushed against my ear as I listened to the ring—once, twice, four times until the answering machine picked up. I did that three times, in rapid succession. I didn't leave a message because how can you leave something like that on an answering machine?

"I've been raped. Call me when you can."

It's not the kind of news that rolls off the tongue and it definitely doesn't feel like something that can be said to the echo chamber of a voicemail tape.

I wish she would have answered. Had I called my parents, they would have driven down the second they heard my voice and I was too ashamed to let them see me in the condition I was in, shaking uncontrollably, keening in a corner. I couldn't bring myself to wake up my friends, the thought of explaining everything to them just felt too large. My sister, that was the phone call I could make, because I knew she would answer. She would sit on the phone with me all night, even if I fell asleep. I knew she would storm the gates of hell to be curled up in the bed beside me in whatever way she could. Except she didn't answer and I was desperately scared.

We have shared everything in our lives. There are few stones left unturned. But we've never talked about that—the unanswered call—but also those incredibly dark hours before I did tell someone. This thing, this unanswered call that we've never talked about hangs in the space between us, I think because we can't make sense of how the sister connection that we had become reliant upon failed us that night. Jessie would say she failed us that night.

Talking about the rape has become a muscle well-exercised. Beyond the years in therapy processing and reprocessing, I have learned how to talk about the rape in constructive ways born out of genuine healing and also self-protection. I've learned the safe ways of talking about it and the ways that my heart and head cannot tolerate. It is easier to talk about this trauma more broadly; to tell the story in familiar chunks. I healed in such a way that enabled me to talk in generalization. It is more difficult to zoom down into the worst moments. I think that's true for many of us who have experienced trauma. No one can live in technicolor memory for too long if they hope to piece back their lives.

The unanswered call is difficult to talk about and because of that, I can only assume that it sits somewhere among the worst moments, but not because I feel mad at Jessie. To be sure, anger at Jessie does not come easily to me. I'm too loyal to her and too wrapped up in my own flaws and mistakes to pile onto the shame and regret that she has already heaped on herself about that call. I think this moment sits like a stone because it was when I first comprehended how alone and helpless I really was. I quickly came to the understanding that whether or not she had picked up the phone did not change that this had happened to only me, not to us, and the sense of isolation was debilitating.

There is a genre of biblical literature known as lament. Lament is found throughout the Bible, but it's most recognizable in the Psalms. Lament is a cry out to God; a voice that gathers strength from the sacred deep within and demands to be heard. There are psalms of communal lament, representing a group or nation, and there are psalms of individual lament. That night, when Jessie didn't answer the phone, the lament was mine alone to bear and only God was there to hear it.

It was like that for a while, really. For about a week, I expended a tremendous amount of energy being okay, able to converse, going to class. And then at night, when the lights were off, the real work began. The keening. The building and cresting of grief and shame, the indignity so thick that it choked out any chance that how I felt could be made known in the daylight hours. The nighttime was the only time when my lament could find its voice.

In the months and years following the rape, I would learn how *not* alone I really was, both through the presence and support of family and friends, Jessie primary among them, but also through the dawning recognition that my voice of lament was just one among countless other survivors. But on that night in 2001, there was only my singular voice, my own lamentation psalm to a God that I hoped was listening.

> *Answer me when I cry out, my righteous God!*
> *Set me free from my troubles! Have mercy on me!*
> *Listen to my prayer!... Know this: the Lord takes*
> *personal care of the faithful. The Lord will hear me*
> *when I cry out to him.* —Psalm 4:1, 3 (CEB)

HER BODY TOLD ME

Jessie

Where was my rage?

That's the number one thing I want to know now. Not the details of that night, or the details of the trial, or the details of his life now, or even the massive gaps in memory from that time. There are so many missing gaps.

I don't remember how many days passed before Dani went into the hospital. I don't remember why on earth I didn't leave school immediately, why I didn't just get on a plane and fly to DC and start sistering the shit out of everything. I don't know why that practical side of my brain tried to just keep doing normal life—go to classes, go to rehearsal, go to my job, just *add* this massive trauma in my sister's life onto the pile of things I was juggling each day. This is how we were trained in my family. You don't quit things, and if you need to quit them you do so only with a clear argument for what you are replacing it with. You would certainly not say, "Well I am going to need several hours per day to talk on the phone and cry and stare at the wall in numb silence, so I'd better adjust my commitments here." Nope. You add it on top of everything else and manage.

I don't remember when I finally did come home. I know it was after Dani checked herself into the hospital. I think I remember Dani and I sitting on the radiator in the dining room. That is the best spot in the house, by the way. It's a rattly old Victorian radiator, just the length of a young woman's body, and you can lie on it and have all that old dry heat go into your back and your legs, your shoulder blades, the back of your head, the bay windows all around you, and still be in the center of the downstairs. I have a memory of Dani and me sitting on the radiator together once she was out of the hospital. I asked my mom if she could confirm this, or if she had any memories of my trip home after the hospital, and she replied in her dreamy cadence, "You came home?"

Fine. All of that is lost. Or stored in some deep fascia tissue down inside my body. If I were going to have a baby maybe those memories would exorcise while my pelvis cracked open and heaved against the contractions. I'd be pushing and suddenly start screaming memories from spring 2001 until whoosh, the crown of a head. But I'm not going to have a baby. So perhaps the intensity of some other malady will force the body to give up its secret files, or maybe that's what deathbeds are for.

What I do remember is grief. Grief through tears, yes. But also grief through silence. Grief through denial. Grief through getting on with life. I moved to New York City immediately after graduating that spring and I remember disagreeing with my boyfriend about turning off our phones at night. What if someone needed us? He said anything someone might call about could wait until the morning. I said he had clearly never gotten that call.

I remember weird grief. Misplaced grief.

Around the same time as the phone call conversation, I had an abnormal pap smear, and my gynecologist wanted to immediately do a colposcopy. A colposcopy is an in-office procedure when the doctor takes a biopsy of the cervix to get a bigger sample of tissue to see if there is dysplasia, if the cells are changing in a pre-cancerous way. My boyfriend offered to come with me to the procedure. But I never want to see another human being after putting my feet in the cold metal stirrups, being cranked open with a metal speculum and poked with instruments. So I declined.

Bad idea.

In case you too need a colposcopy one day, let me be the first to tell you: It hurts. They put a little set of teeth up to your cervix and take a big ol' bite. I *howled*. I hyperventilated. My top lip buzzed and then went numb. I panicked. They had no idea what to do with me. And then despite not finding much evidence of dysplasia but fueled by a certainty that HPV must be eradicated before you're even sure it's there, they decided I should have a LEEP, a surgical procedure to remove and cauterize a small portion of the cervical opening.

When I had to schedule the day off with the rich lady on the Upper East Side whose daughters I nanny-ed, she suggested I get a second opinion, and deep down I knew she was right. (They never did find HPV, all of this was for nothing.) But I somehow couldn't bear that. I felt overwhelmed. I was twenty-three and absolutely broke and auditioning for acting jobs and sometimes getting them while working three other jobs. So I went forward with the surgery at a hospital on the East Side. Because of my level of distress from the colposcopy, they put me under general anesthesia. I remember being wheeled into the surgery room in little medical booties and the cotton gown. The anesthesiologist told me to count down from ten and I remember getting to seven.

I tell this story now because from the vantage point of the years passed, I just see grief. I was ringing with it. Howling it out when a doctor did a simple biopsy procedure. I imagine the doctors thinking, "Holy shit! Something is clearly wrong with her! Let's go in and cauterize the cervix. The perpetual wound that all women walk around with? Let's just numb that right down. She'll thank us." Maybe I was cuing them—*it's here, it hurts here. Get it out of me. Find it and remove it and definitely cauterize all around it. Just make it stop hurting.*

What was the *it*? That someone hurt Dani. That someone brutalized her. Humiliated her. Blamed her. Shamed her. In secret. And then in public. Someone took her away from herself. From us. For *years*. Not forever, thank God, I can say that now.

She would later say it was like a ghost walking beside her. The rape. The traumatized self. A ghost walking beside her. And this is true. For many, many months after the rape, Dani was there but not there. She was out of focus. Grainy. Beneath the blurry lines of her shape was the feeling of something sharp. Like shards of glass. I was terrified of her. I experienced it as aimed at me. Blame. I tried to ignore it. To just be with her. To go on as Jessie and Dani.

But where was my rage?

Perhaps that is my greatest failure in this story. Not that I missed the phone call, or even that it took Dani going into the hospital for me to fly home. But that I didn't feel rage. Grief was safer.

About a month-and-a-half after the rape, Dani and her friend Kelly came to Boston for their spring break. I had to go to Los Angeles and New York for my graduating class's showcase, a grotesque and crucial part of any actor training when you introduce yourself to the industry by parading across a stage and showing you can get work and make money. But I was able to be in Boston with them for several days and then they stayed on in my room for the rest of their spring break and I flew west.

Kelly was in the shower and Dani was napping in my bed. I was sitting on the bed, putting on my shoes, when I suddenly felt something enter the room.

I stopped and looked up to my door, which was closed, and of course nothing was there. I turned and looked at Dani, still sleeping absolutely soundly. *Huh*.

So I continued putting on my shoes.

But I could not shake this feeling—an absolutely physical certainty—*something is here now*. I looked back at the door and then back at Dani... and I waited. Within a count of ten, her flashback began.

It started very small. Her hands were gently closed in little fists and they began to twitch. Her breathing became tight.

And then it grew.

Her legs began to move, like a treading motion, like she was in a huge body of water... And I knew what was happening. I had talked to Dani every day since the rape, multiple times per day (a tradition that continues to this day). Her flashbacks came daily, mostly while she was sleeping, but sometimes during class or in the dining hall. I can't imagine that now. How awful it must have been for Dani, to know her body was telling anyone and everyone her truth, telling them without her permission. So I knew what I was seeing. And this is odd to say now, but I had this distinct sense that I should let the flashback take its course.

I'd been reading about PTSD, how when a trauma occurs there can be a splintering of the self. Some say that it's the self before the trauma and the self inside the trauma, and they're trying to reconcile each other. To see each other, hear each other, to integrate. I told myself this was Dani's body and soul trying to heal itself. This was necessary and important. So at first I didn't make sound. I sat next to her and I let it go.

But very quickly the treading intensified. Her breath couldn't get in. I became distressed with her. I wanted her to know it wasn't really happening, that it was a bad dream, so I said, "Dani, I'm here. You're safe."

But my voice didn't wake her. I thought surely she'd wake up as soon as I spoke. I thought my voice would break the spell. I became frightened. And her legs kept treading and treading, like she was trying to outswim a wave that was already upon her. She's kicked herself up against the wall. Her face . . . I don't know how to describe her face. She's started making a muffled sound, the struggle intensifying.

I said, louder, "Dani? Can you hear me? It's Jessie. I'm here with you."

But the wave was on her now, overwhelming her. I thought, "Enough!" I reached out to touch her. She recoiled from me. Like I was him. Like my touch burned her. And she let out this closed-mouth scream—like a little bunny, like someone was clamping her mouth, and it was then that I understood:

I wasn't here. She wasn't here. She was *there*. She was with him.

I couldn't reach her. I was powerless. She had to live through it all over again. Suddenly all my reading on PTSD seemed like a bunch of psychology bullshit. The body wasn't healing itself. The body was being tortured. Again. Because people are not supposed to endure these things and the body can't tolerate it. Like a fever when the temperature is too high from infection, the body tries to *exhume*.

I kept repeating, helplessly, uselessly, "Dani, I'm here. I'm with you. I'm here."

Eventually, her legs slowed. The wave receded and beached her sunken body on the bed. Her fists twitched a little longer and then stopped. Maybe a minute later she woke up. I asked if she remembered having a bad dream. She nodded yes.

How could I have gotten on a plane to Los Angeles after that? How could I have worn make up and matched my shoes to my pants and rehearsed a comedic scene? How could I possibly have given a shit about anything after that?

I remember our brother saying he wanted to get a group of friends together and go down to DC and beat the shit out of him. I was like, *Ugh. Violence for violence, Chip? Come on, dude.* But you know what? That was a healthy response. Chip felt rage. Where was mine?

And what about now? Do I feel rage now?

Yes. Something like rage pulls inside me. Like a web of thin strings hooked from my xiphoid process to my temples, my brow, rage pulls these strings and I feel myself curl in. I fantasize about finding Yuri. He probably still lives in the DC area. He probably drives an Audi. A black one. With leather interior. I imagine following him home from work. Past monuments that articulate the American experiment of freedom and choices. I watch him pick up one of his kids from school. Then he pulls up and gets takeout for family dinner. Then he drives home, the implacable Washington Monument fading in the rearview mirror as he glides across the bridges and rounded parkways into the suburbs with their thick, verdant trees and softer air. He pulls into the shiny driveway of a big McMansion. The kid runs ahead inside. He takes his time, gathering his brief case and the takeout. And that's when I get out of my car. I walk right up to him. He feels me approach and stops. Turns around. And sees me. His eyes are still like bruises. He isn't sure who I am. Until I start speaking. If people are ever not sure if Dani and I are sisters, it only takes one word out of our mouths and then the cadences are so similar there can be no doubt. He knows who I am. Why I'm there. His face goes pale. And then...

And then...

I don't know. Suddenly my rage fails me. Buckles. The fantasy instantly crumbles. Suddenly I'm just sitting on the edge of my bed. Unable to reach Dani. Unable to stop it. Suddenly I'm sleeping while the phone rings. And rings again. And rings again. As if my failures are tied to his and I have no right to punish him if I have my own. I don't know.

I don't know how to end this.

I don't know how it ends.

PEOPLE KNOW ABOUT MY BODY

Dani

I'm standing in my bedroom, a pair of leggings on and my comfy bra. I'm home from work and I had made a direct line from my car to my bedroom to don what I wear when I'm not killing it in my wedges and pedal-pusher pants. It's an awkward dance mentally. I wear what I wear in the day as part of the armor of confidence I put on to face the day. I wear makeup to enhance my features and hide my fatigue. There's probably a book to be written about why I feel the need to do this, but mostly, I'm comfortable with my vanity and my battle against fine lines. But that moment when I get home is so critical because it's part of my mental shift, when I back away from the composure I have held throughout the day and move into the comfort of being off-duty. I just really want to wear pants that don't restrict and cardigans that are ugly and ratty but warm.

Alan has just left to go pick up takeout and I can hear the panic in Grace's voice when she cries out to me, "Mommy?" She's worried that I left with him. "I'm right here. I'm up here." She climbs the steps and pads down the hallway. "Oh you're here," she says cheerfully. "You're dressing your body?" I've bent down now to be eye-to-eye with her and her tiny hands start patting my chest. Not hard—gentle like a pat on the back but instead, placing them in that space where my rib cage meets my clavicle. "This is your body. Do you love your body, Mommy?" My breath catches. For a moment, I cannot speak.

People know about my body.

Something that no one tells you about lady-pastoring is that people are forever commenting on your body. They notice when you gain weight or when your hair is different.

They notice and comment when you look tired. When you're pregnant, they notice if you are carrying high or low, and implicit in their noticing of your pregnant body is the knowledge that you had sex to make it that way. I've grown accustomed to my parishioners noticing what I'm wearing. Some women fight the patriarchy with Keens, hairy legs, and natural deodorant; some of us fight it in a brightly colored heel. To each their own.

My husband Alan knows that he can't put his arms around me from behind. On TV shows when a husband walks into a room and his wife is cooking, he puts his arms around her waist and kisses her neck. Alan tried to do that once early in our marriage and he ended up with a fat lip.

I once did an exercise where I recalled the sexual encounters that I had with men. I started back with the boyfriends from high school, though truthfully, I could have started back when an adult rubbed my shoulders when I was in the sixth grade. My parents were never the types to offer us a narrative of shame about our bodies. They never told us if we were skinny or fat or something else. They encouraged us to eat and didn't make comments over what we chose to eat. But when I look back over the years, it seems that culturally that shame was baked into me. That cultural narrative that women's bodies were meant to be consumed, paired with the familial narrative that I was responsible for pleasing everyone was the perfect combination to make me doubt the truth of my own experience over the years. A touchy adult, a boy who would whisper graphic things to me in math class, a boyfriend who hit me—I accumulated mistreatment and filed it somewhere between "that's just the way it is" and "I must have provoked him."

Looking back, it can sometimes feel like all those experiences were leading up to meeting Yuri. I met him in one of my first classes at American University. It was a cinema class, some gen-ed that had us watch old movies and write papers about them. Our professor was a survivor of the Holocaust, and he had an affinity for the brooding guy in the front row. Yuri, also a survivor of genocide, had come to the United States a refugee and had forged a life here going to school. We were assigned to do a project together and from there we became friends. It was easy enough to be friends with Yuri.

He was a well of pain and experience, and I was a bucket of empathy, a vessel he could share with. We spent a lot of time going on walks late at night. He was older than me and certainly more mature and so our daytime lives didn't intersect much. He had an actual job, not just a work-study, and he hung out with older people. But evenings we would go for walks all around campus, breaking into fenced-off soccer fields or lying on the steps of the amphitheater. He never said so, but I think the nights were hard for him because there never seemed to be any limit to how late he was willing to stay together. He'd lay his head in my lap and ask me to recount stories from my childhood or tell him about what it was like to grow up in a small town in America. He used to say that he thought I could talk to the animals, like some kind of Disney character. Our childhoods were quite different.

He didn't share much about his life, just snippets about his parents or his siblings. I remember one night in the fall of 2000, he came to my room and was bereft. "The wrong person won." He was referring to the election of Slobodan Milosevic in Yugoslavia. I was only nineteen and ridiculously sheltered. At the time, it was early in our friendship and I had no way of fully understanding how truly devastating that election was for him, an ethnic Albanian; I only knew that he sought my comfort and I hated to see him in such pain. Yuri struggled to talk about what he endured growing up in Kosovo, but I remember he shared that he and his family had been rounded up by the Serbian army and that they had endured abuse and trauma, in particular his sister.

I don't believe that if pain is inflicted on us that we necessarily inflict pain on others, but I do believe that's often the case. Unresolved pain begets more pain. In the trial, months after he had raped me, Yuri was asked if I had cried out, if I had fought him, if I said no. Yes, he said. I had cried out. I had kicked him. I had yelled no. After hearing his answer, the follow up question was asked, "Do you think you raped her?" He responded with an emphatic, "No." Twenty years later, and I still think he really believed his own words.

How do you trust your own experience when years upon years have told you that what other people say and do is more important?

My experience was this: I loved Yuri and wanted him to love me. I wanted to take his pain and wrap it in a thousand warm blankets and cradle it between us. I wanted to be the innocence and the purity and the goodness that he craved. But I didn't want to have sex with him. I liked kissing him, I liked holding him. I liked the way he held my face or put his hand on the small of my back. I liked that he wanted to be close to me, but I also knew, in some deeply instinctual way, that he was a person whose pain would beget pain. I thought that meant that he would break up with me.

What it really meant was that one cold night in February he came to my room and raped me. What started as a slow but persistent disregard for my redirection of his hands eventually culminated in my legs pinned open under each of his knees, my mouth gasping for air under the weight of his shoulder pressing on my face, a U2 song playing in the background, my hands pressing and smacking him, my voice pleading.

The thing about rape is this: in that moment and forever afterward, people know something about my body that I did not grant. They have a story about my body that I didn't give them. That story gets told, over and over again, through hospital reports and psychologist notes, by friends and a family who care and need to process with one another, and even by me. But it's not a story about my body that I chose; it is a story about my body that was forced upon me but is now forever my body story.

I have no memory of how I spent the day after the rape, I only know that that evening, I took myself to the emergency room and the story that other people tell about my body began. It started with the phone call where I had to tell my father so that he would understand the emergency room bill. Next came the receptionist as she inquired what had brought me in, which prompted a conversation with the triage nurse. It could be that the laws in DC are different than they were in 2001, but at that time, when a person came into the emergency room because of sexual assault, the first thing that happened was not a physical exam. There was no offer of a blanket or even a rape counselor. The first thing they did was put you in a windowless room, a former broom closet, with a small table, a folding chair, and a telephone.

Entirely utilitarian, this room was to be the space where I had to decide whether or not I wanted a rape kit.

The decision was not as simple as one might expect. A rape kit came with a call to DC Police. There were not rape kits without the police. If I got a rape kit, the exam by the physician would be centered around evidence collection and once done, the process of prosecution would continue, whether or not I want to press charges. The evidence collected from my body would now be considered property of the state. If I didn't get a rape kit, my ability to press charges still existed, but no longer included the evidence gathering afforded by a rape kit. The weight of that choice still hangs on me now, twenty years later. Even then I knew that it was a statistical probability that the person who raped me would rape again. Even then I knew that the particular history of my rapist, a refugee from a country whose government was literally committing acts of genocide against its citizens, would mean that a crime committed threatened deportation, return to a country where he could be murdered. It seemed all my training as a child had come to fruition in this moment. What was my body worth? Was it worth a person's life? Was it worth his life? How would this decision impact him? My family?

My parents did the best they could when I called them to make this decision with me. Did I really want people to know about my body? In the end, I answered no. But the truth is, people already knew about my body. From those early moments with the receptionist, continuing with each nurse and doctor and professor and attorney and counselor—on and on—each person I had to tell about my body in order to make it through the next year of my life without flunking out of college. So many conversations about my body.

When the doctor did my exam, he nodded his head solemnly as he lined up the instruments that would aid his inspection—a vaginal speculum, swabs, and bright lights. There was no turning back now; people were going to know about my body. The doctor chronicled the exam and my injuries on a medical record. At the top left corner of the page, there was the outline of a body, meant to represent my body. Bruise here. Tearing there. Trauma. Maybe a word or two about my reaction to being touched. Final assessment: sexual assault. I think that's where the autonomy of my body, which he had stolen, became codified—on that black outline of a body that was supposed to be me. Of all the conversations that were to be had about my body, that room heard not a word from me—but my body told them anyway.

So people know about my body now.

Two days after I was raped, one day after the hospital, I went to the healing service that was held in the university chapel every Thursday evening. After prayers and quiet songs, the congregation was invited forward to be anointed with oil and to have healing prayers said over you. I remember walking to the altar rail, the chaplain walking over to me and asking why I was being anointed, for what could he be praying? I told him that something had been taken from me. That night in February, I had no idea just how much had been taken from me. I had no idea that within the month I would be making plans to kill myself. I had no idea that months after that, I'd still be cutting myself. I had no idea that I would develop PTSD, or that I would face my attacker in a room before a jury of my peers. I had no way of knowing the little, infinitesimal ways that I would change my life and way of being in the world to accommodate this new reality—that my body was no longer mine alone. People would know about my body and because of that, I would no longer experience my body as a home but instead as a prison, a prison that I so fiercely wanted to be free of.

There are lots of things that I could say right now to spin this into a story of empowerment. I have therapied the shit out of this experience. I am a professional at making meaning out of terrible things. That is literally one of my primary jobs as a pastor—to make meaning out of the traumatic and terrible, to find grace and resurrection in the ashes. I believe in that ministry. I believe God can transform heartache. I do. I know that one of the reasons I can access a well of empathy when folks are in pain is because of my own experiences of such pain. And to be sure, there is grace and meaning and resurrection that comes out of the story of my rape—but before there is any of that, and even after there is any of that, there is one true thing that stands as a pillar: people know a story about my body that I did not give them permission to have. I did not give them permission to have it because in the end, I did not give my permission to him—he took it. He has a story about my body that I did not grant him.

There is no way to dress that up or make it better. This body, which is my own and no one else's, now shares a narrative with a rapist. This body shares a narrative with every person who was ever on the "need to know" list of people I had to tell whether for my own healing or for theirs. This body shares a narrative with the one in four women who experience rape.

This body shares a narrative—people know about my body. And now, I guess, so do you.

But at this moment in my bedroom, my three-year-old daughter patting me gently, asking me with her whole sweet face if I love my body… She does not know. She does not know about my body.

In truth, I don't like my body, but I'm at peace with my body. I don't know when I stopped obsessing over the shape and size of my body—but my feelings about my body changed over time with bearing children. Part of it, I think, is that I just feel too busy to think about my body too much. But it's something more than that. I think I'm starting to see my body the way my kids do—as home.

When Sam was somewhere between two and three years old, I asked him if he remembered being in my belly. I asked him that because I'd heard this theory that children this young still retain something of their utero experience. I didn't think he'd actually answer.

"It was warm, like my bed," he said. Knowing Sam now, knowing him as the thirteen-year-old empath that he is, I am not the least bit surprised that something from being in my belly imprinted on him. But back then, it took my breath away. I asked him, "and do you remember my talking to you?" "Oh yes," he said.

"And what did you do?"

"I kick, kick, kicked you!" And he did. He really did kick me when I spoke to him in my belly.

From the time he was born until about eight years old, Sam twirled or played with my hair. He did it to fall asleep; he did it when he was anxious; he did it when he was relaxing on the couch. His fingers would always find their way to my head and he'd start taking my curls apart and weaving them in and out of his fingers.

Liam stayed in my belly until I evicted him. Two weeks after his due date. Even his induction took forever. He took his good, sweet time getting out.

The second night in the hospital after having him, he cried almost nonstop. Alan was home with Sam and I was sure I could handle being alone at the hospital. But his incessant crying brought me to tears. The nurse came in and saw my desperation.

"He's just realizing he's not inside of you. This happens on the second night like this—they just sort of come awake to the fact that they are out in the world." She recommended that I take the nursing camisole I was wearing, open it up, and put him in there like a little papoose or cocoon—from that spot on the chest, a baby can hear and feel your heartbeat, which was their soundtrack in your belly. I was skeptical when she told me, but I was so tired that I agreed. And damn if he didn't stay there all night happy, interchanging nursing with sleeping in the sphere of protection on my bosom.

And that's the way he's been ever since. There are times when Liam is cuddling or we are in our night-night routine when I feel like he is trying to crawl back into my womb. He wants to be surrounded by my voice and warmth.

And then there's Grace. Grace who wants to be near me but not held by me. Grace whose independence bursts out of her and ricochets off every surface and person she encounters. Grace doesn't want or need to be enveloped by anything or anyone—she wants to lead *you*, guide *you* to what she *does* need. Often attention or conversation or affirmation, but rarely a cuddle.

So when she pats my chest and tells me she loves my body, that my body is great—it sort of breaks me open. Because why? Why would she love my body? I didn't know it, but I think some part of me wondered if she had already been judging my body—the way we fear all women judge our bodies. I wondered if that had already taken root in her.

But of course she hasn't been judging my body. She just holds up my shirt and says things like, "look at this BIG shirt! Put on this BIG SHIRT, Mommy." Because she thinks it's great. Because she's twenty pounds and anything bigger than that is BIG. Any other meaning assigned to "big" is entirely my own. And she's only two so it must be fleeting, but her ease with my body and the confidence with which she moves in her own make me proud.

There is so much of who she will be (and already is) that I can take no credit for, that I have nothing to do with—but this, I want to hold as something. That I've managed to celebrate her body and my own body enough that she says it's great. God, I hope that that assurance and joy and acceptance follow her or rest in her in a way that has escaped me until recently. I don't really like my body—but I do take joy in my body.

This body that housed three children, grew them from embryo to infant and pushed them into the world. This body that was broken by assaulters and loved back to wholeness by my husband. This body whose ovaries quit at thirty-nine—just threw in the towel and said, "no more." This body that will house my soul until the last breath.

We say it in the church a lot—that ours is an embodied faith. We worship a God who we say literally became flesh and dwelt among us. We worship a God whose body was birthed and grew and sweat and stunk and tread and was broken. So why should I dislike mine so much?

It strikes me that in this embodied faith, I've been called—entrusted—to be with people as they inhabit their bodies—as they enter the world in their bodies and leave their bodies behind in their death, and so much in between.

I'm standing in a surgical room in a hospital on the South Side of Chicago. It's 2005. I've been scrubbed in to go into the room where the surgery is happening—I'm in full scrubs, shower cap, face masks, fully gloved. In my hand is a tiny tube with sterilized water, the top cracked open.

What brought me to that room was a few weeks in the making. I'd met Maria on the labor and delivery floor where she had been a patient, awaiting the birth of her son,

Manuel—who had a severe heart anomaly. It was unclear whether Manuel would survive the birth, but if he did, as soon as he left his mother's womb, he would go into surgery. In the preceding weeks, as the chaplain intern for that floor of the hospital, I had met with Maria on a number of occasions, and though she spoke only Spanish, we found a way to communicate. Mostly, I just sat with her and held her hand and prayed. When the time came for the scheduled c-section, Maria wanted to be sure that her son was baptized before he went into the surgery.

It took some doing—but because of the situation, the doctors were committed to honoring her wishes. So that's how I ended up in the surgical theatre that morning, with the sterilized water in my hand, ready to baptize Manuel. I watched as Manuel was pulled from his Mama and with the signal of the doctors, with a nurse beside me, I cradled Manuel and baptized him, "En el nombre del Padre, y del Hijo, y del Espiritu Santo"—in the name of the Father, the Son, and Holy Spirit, said loud enough so his Mama could hear it. It was the first baptism I had ever done... and I don't speak a word of Spanish—but I wanted Maria to hear the words I said to her son. No matter what happened that day or in the days to come, it was important to Maria that she hear and know, this beautiful child was named and claimed by God.

Manuel lived for just a week after he was born.

And I suspect that the primary reason that Maria wanted Manuel baptized was because of her Catholic faith, a belief that this Christening was paramount in her son's salvation. But I wondered if it was also something more. A mother's desire that her child's life, however brief, would be marked by more than medical equipment.

When I think of my time in ministry—I rarely think of prayers I've said. My words just aren't that memorable. I rarely think of money raised or programs started.

When I look back, what I remember are bodies. Hands with paper thin skin and blue veins; a body crouched over a toilet, heaving after chemotherapy; the softness of peach fuzz that covers a newborn's body; the strength of a child on the soccer field; the coolness of a body recently departed; the warmth of a body tucked under covers. I'm struck that in all of these moments there has not been embarrassment or shame or fear—but rather this incredible willingness to let me see—and be near—the body they inhabit—good, bad, ugly or otherwise. Because the body—it really is great. It's our home. The home of our loves and our memories and our learning and our time on the earth.

"This is your body. Do you love your body, Mommy?" Grace smiles up at me expectantly. And before I can respond she says, "I love your body, mommy. Your body is great."

And I can feel what she means, the way she's laid her hands on me. She really does love my body. And in that moment, inside the gaze of her love, I do too.

She picks out a shirt for me and we walk downstairs together.

BABIES

Jessie

Dani barely screamed when she gave birth to Sammy. Or any of her three children. This is really saying something considering when Dani was a baby she was a champion screamer. So voluminous and piercing was her cry that as a family we nicknamed it her Ultimate Weapon. If baby Dani was displeased, she let you know. She'd open her mouth and that big gun was unleashed. But while delivering her own babies, Dani kept those screams clenched tight between her teeth.

That first delivery I tried to hang back. I felt I was just lucky to be there. I was only a few weeks away from opening my playwriting debut Off-Broadway. The baby was due during the run of the show, and I had designed an entire contingency plan for the moment she went into labor. How I would finish the show and jump into a rental car (all locations within two miles of the theater thoroughly scouted and saved in my phone) and drive through the night to get to the hospital, hopefully in time to be of some use to her, or to relieve Alan at her side.

Before rehearsals began, I took the train from New York City to Pennsylvania to visit and Dani wasn't feeling great. The previous week her liver enzymes were up in the blood work, and she had been instructed to take her blood pressure every hour and be on bed rest, keeping a watch out for pain in the upper quadrant of her abdomen.

By the time I arrived on Sunday, she had the pain and her blood pressure kept going up and up. Her OB-GYN told her to go straight to the hospital to be checked. This was literally a full month before she was due. We never went home. They diagnosed her with pre-eclampsia and a rare syndrome called HELLP. HELLP affects the blood and the liver and can cause fatal seizures for the mother. The labor was immediately induced. They put her on magnesium sulfate to help prevent the seizures, but the result is an intense flu-like feeling. As if having your vagina splayed open wasn't terrible enough, here's the flu while we monitor how close you are to dying. After waiting so long for this moment to arrive, it was suddenly upon us, and with dark clouds overhead.

It was a slow, harrowing string of hours as the Pitocin dripped down into her veins and commanded her cervix to gape. I paced the hospital hall. What was this? I knew labor would be difficult, but life threatening? Dani was descending into a strange fever dream of moans. Moans strangely high and stifled by her cheeks and teeth. The doctor was not the OB-GYN she knew, and he was dry, clinical. I felt angry. She was in acute pain and discomfort. People were coming in and out of the room and no one seemed to care. The doctor would just check, see the cervix wasn't dilated enough, and leave again. It's not that they weren't paying attention. It was a dangerous situation, and they were coming in and out of the room constantly, but there was nothing to be done but wait and hope it didn't get worse.

Alan, my parents, and I hovered helplessly. We hung around her room like limp coats. We had no idea how to be. I remember surveying the scene and suddenly having a frightening thought: *No one is at the wheel*. We were all just passengers on this ship. No one was *navigating*. My mother had gone through labor. Three times! But she too seemed lost as to what could help her youngest daughter. She just sat in a chair and tried to read a book. At least that's what I remember. She wasn't disinterested, she was helpless; she was coping. We were all trying to stay out of the way of the medical team while this endless process wended its torturous way to the only part we had previously let ourselves imagine—Dani holding our beautiful Sammy in her arms. The nurses had a change of shift, the old useless one left, the new useless one entered. She was dark blond, already tired, padding around in pale pink scrubs. Dani was letting out little yips of pain, and not one of them even blinked. I felt Dani going away. Her audible pain surrounded by the fog of everyone's silence (the medical staff's task-oriented silence, and our task-*less* silence) seemed to draw her deeper down into despair.

I left the room to pace the hall again. I suddenly understood women were at the mercy of a terrible complicity. Told that labor is beautiful, motherhood is a gift, and everyone who does it is a hero. I thought, "This is total bullshit! You wanna have a baby, ladies? Cool. But make no mistake—you are risking your life." A mysterious, enormous door was creaking open, and a new person, a new soul, was going to come through. But only Dani could approach that door and receive it. I pictured her arms outstretched, reaching into the threshold of darkness, waiting for Sammy to land there. But I suddenly understood with absolute certainty that just as he could come out from the darkness,

Dani could fall through. That portal was two-way and the rest of us who love her and need her more than anyone or anything on the other side of that darkness are standing down below her in a befuddled fog of cold, medical light trying to figure out how to snap out of our anesthetized haze and *help her*. She needed a lifeline, and I didn't know what else to do except what I had always tried to do since 1981: Be the lifeline.

I don't fully trust my memory here, but I know a thought pierced through the fog like a lighthouse strobe—*I will take the wheel*. I know *zero* about labor or medicine, but I hurled myself toward that wheel and pulled hard. Which started with that poor pink-scrub nurse. I told her that my sister was in pain and I needed her to *respond* to my sister's pain. *Right now*. Then I started staring at the monitor of Dani's contractions, trying to teach myself how to coach her through them so she would understand when they were coming and when they were going. I wanted to give her the ability to actively participate in her own coping. I was probably doing everything wrong but I didn't care. At least I was doing something.

Dani did finally dilate enough and she began to push. I remember imagining Dani beginning her descent down from that enormous, treacherous door. Sammy's arm was hooked around his head, kinda like he was lounging on a beanbag propping himself up to read. This is why he had been stuck and the dilation had been slow. Then the doctor finally gave a *helpful* statement—he told Dani to push like she was pooping. I saw her eyes light up, *"Now THAT, I can do,"* and suddenly the progress went quickly. Dani pulled Sammy through that veil of darkness and they both emerged back to us safely. The room felt filled with light. I was suddenly back on board with the whole shenanigan. Birth was a miracle. Motherhood was a gift. Dani was a hero.

Her next two pregnancies would be labeled High Risk, since there is something like a forty-percent chance of recurrence of HELLP. But with each delivery after Sammy—Liam and then Gracie—it got better and better.

Dani moved to York for her first church and found a new OB-GYN, this time a midwife—a petite firecracker who strode into the delivery room in four-inch heels and a pencil skirt, with the vocal swagger of a field hockey coach. When the time came for Dani to deliver and the midwife pulled out a huge bottle of what looked like olive oil and poured it all over Dani's vagina, I thought, "I *like* this woman."

Through Liam, Dani's constant incantation was, "This is so much better than the first time!" And it was. I remember the moment Liam's little nose popped out we shouted like a touchdown. He was two weeks late and enormous and jolly and we bathed him in the sound of our collective heaving and contracting and cheering. We rode up and down every contraction with Dani, we massaged her back, we fed her popsicles, we watched movies. I suspect she felt much more held.

By the time it was Gracie's turn we were *pros* and I knew my role. I had to keep being bossy, politely reminding the nurse for the fifth time that we would still really love that cup of ice, pressing pause on *Bridesmaids* so I could delicately carry all Dani's IV cords and machine behind her into the bathroom so she could pee, pulling her underwear down and then back up, all while narrating in some stupid accent to try to make her laugh.

Dani is the one who takes care of everyone around her. She's the rock. Dani is competent and cheerfully commanding, and she manages her own suffering so privately and completely, that it's easy to think, *She's got this*.

When Dani was considering whether to stay at the school where she was raped, I had no idea what she should do. So, I just tried to be supportive. Why should she have to evacuate the place she chose to study of all the schools she got into? She hadn't done anything wrong, why should she be punished and have to leave? Why should she take another loss? In hindsight, Dani needed help letting go. Permission to cry "uncle" and go make a fresh start. But a deeply instilled financial pragmatism, plus a devotion to the family scripture "Quitting Is for Losers," kept her at American University. I had tried to be a thought partner, whatever she wanted. I think I was trying to let her have her own choice, since the events that led to this choice were a moment of her having absolutely, violently, *none*. But now I can see that I was frightened. I wanted to be fooled. Dani? *She's got this.*

There is a lesson both of our adult selves could have whispered back to us: It's okay to call it. You don't have to loyally see this through, carry on and make everything work. *There is also strength in walking away*. But it would take many years and failures to learn that, and our future selves stayed silent this time.

Over the years, Dani has realized she has trouble saying what she needs. She can talk to you for twenty minutes about what this has to do with her Enneagram type (and I can make fun of her for that), but by the time Dani had her legs in stirrups pushing out babies, she has gotten better at saying her needs, and I'd gotten better at anticipating them. With baby three we had it *down*.

Dani is who taught me how to deeply be with someone. Because this is what she does with her parishioners. It's her superpower. And as each of those little faces I watched come out of her body have grown, I've seen her do this with them—deeply *be* with them—from their middle-of-the-night tears, to their scholastic victories, or schoolyard losses, or just bad moods. Dani furrows her brow in the way she does when she's listening intently and says, "Tell me."

What's that Bible quote? "Here I am, God. Send me." For Dani? Send me. Every time. Maybe Dani is my god. Or something about her teaches me about the love the Bible is trying to illustrate. Dani has inspired the kind of love that makes me say, "Send me."

NOT A MOTHER

Dani

My sister is not a mother.

She is *maternal*. She is kind, caring, compassionate, loving. She is empathic, self-sacrificing, protective. She is strong, intuitive, responsive. But she is not a mother.

I feel scared to say that. It somehow sounds like an insult, as though being a mother were the pinnacle of what makes a woman. It is not an insult. One can certainly be a mother and not have children. One can certainly have children and not be a mother.

I first realized that Jessie would not have children when she was in college. I wasn't certain of course, but when I peered into the periscope, I could not see a little replica Jessie, with untamed hair and giant blue eyes. I couldn't see a little Jessie playing tea party or creating worlds of play that her adults would indulge. Our family ended up getting a little Jessie—wild hair and all. She came from my body, but she is the mirror image of my sister.

It isn't that I thought Jessie *couldn't* be a mother and it isn't that I thought she *shouldn't* be a mother. It just seemed clear to me that she wouldn't. Despite mothering me my whole life, I felt with certainty she would not choose that path for herself because her life's work required such intense commitment, such singular focus that it felt to me that being presented with the choice of whether to be a mother or be an artist, Jessie would choose artist every time. What she wanted to give birth to, from wholly inside herself, was a life of creativity and beauty, and though that can include children, for Jessie, it wouldn't.

There are people who do both, of course, but I would also say that I have never met a person who has chosen both motherhood and career who has felt that they could be fully and wholly both at the same time. This is an omnipresent truth in my own life. This constant sense of never doing all the things well, all the time. At one time, I had a therapist who told me frequently that "you cannot have it all. There will always be one thing that will take more of you. Some days it will be your children. Some days it will be your work. Some days (though much rarer) it may even be yourself. But you cannot have it all, and if you try to you will be perpetually unhappy." She didn't mean that you had to choose one or the other. She meant that every day you will have to choose who gets more of you. The path Jessie was creating for herself would eliminate the torture of having to make that choice. I know this was not without cost to her. There are no easy choices or answers when it comes to how we live our lives, but it is clear to me that Jessie found many ways to mother without birthing a child. She births so many other things of equal importance.

When Jessie writes a play she starts with a vision. It's always cloudy at first: the outline of a character, or an article that she read on a completely unexpected topic. Sometimes it's what she calls her "fantasy"—just an imaginary scenario that came to her while she was drinking her coffee. From there, she nurtures that idea, she researches it, she lets it simmer and marinate and develop. And then overtime, it shifts and shapes and then months later, I find myself in a theater, weeping or laughing or pondering this play she has written, its characters fresh and developed and nuanced. I look around at the theater full of people and think, "She created this thing and people pay to benefit from its wisdom or laugh at its humor or be challenged by its ideas. The set, designed and built by creative minds and hands. The cast, carefully selected. All of them paid. Because she wrote this thing. She brought it into the world from a seed of an idea in her brain and now it has a life all its own. She labored it into the world."

When Jessie welcomes a guest, she puts fresh flowers by their bedside. She has your favorite drink in the refrigerator. She asks you every day if you'd "like a little nap?" She is highly focused on keeping you hydrated. She is ridiculously gracious and accommodating. She thrives in the caretaking, the nurturing. She delights in your comfort.

When Jessie was at the birth of my children, she rubbed my back. She asked questions about what I wanted or needed. She barked orders at nurses or buttered them up for extra ice and pillows. She helped me shower. When we got home, she woke up with me in the middle of night while I was nursing and didn't flinch when I cried uncontrollably, hormones whooshing out of me on the fourth or fifth day postpartum. She was among the very first faces my children saw—maybe even before mine.

She hosts writing workshops and classes where she nurtures and encourages the writing of others. She follows her kitty cat around the house and makes little beds for their comfort. She talks to her plants and draws little pictures of them with instructions on how to water them. She writes countless notes of encouragement to friends and new acquaintances detailing their gifts and what she sees in them. She reads my sermons every single week.

My sister is not a mother, but she is maternal, and she's more than that. My sister doesn't just birth things, she pulls them into existence; she draws them out and fans their flames. She nurtures ideas and feelings and inspirations. She delivers life and truth and goodness. And most remarkably, she does this for herself, for her own fulfillment, but she also does it for others. Jessie labors alongside so many others so that at the most critical moments, they aren't alone. They are drawn out. They are held. They are welcomed.

My sister is not a mother. My sister is a midwife.

THE FENCE

Jessie

I got off the train at Paoli, where my husband was performing in a play. I intended to tell him everything—the series of searing revelations that I knew would mean a reckoning in our marriage. I didn't know what would happen. We had hit hard times before. We were on our third couples' counselor. We'd always weathered our troubles with truth telling and a genuine desire to see the best in each other, to *believe* the best in each other. But I had not slept in days and I was terrified. As I gathered my travel bag and prepared to deboard the train, the phone cocked between my ear and my shoulder, Dani joked, "Whelp. Call if you need me to come get you!"

Two hours later I would be standing on the street, clutching that same travel bag, arching toward any oncoming headlights, one of which would eventually be Dani and her husband Alan. They had left the table of an anniversary dinner and driven an hour to scrape me off the pavement, put my pieces in their minivan, and drive me back to the safety of their living room. I remember holding their son Liam (then only eight months old) and knowing I would not have children of my own. I had walked away from that life. I was staring into an unmarked wilderness.

At that moment, I texted my brother that I needed to see him first thing the next morning.

In the beginning, Chip Dickey had a good life. Flanked by poor, hippie parents and the family's old English sheepdog, Soltzen Nitzen, Little Chip played in the back alleys and woods of rural Pennsylvania. He rode his dirt bike. He played with G.I. Joe. Then just before his fifth birthday, disaster struck: He had a sister.

There is photographic evidence of Chip enjoying this new member of the family. In one such photo, I am two, wearing a Super Woman outfit. Chip, almost seven, stands behind me, holding the cape aloft so it looks like I am flying. In another picture, we are in the bathtub. But by the time there is a third Dickey child in the family photos, also a girl, I have gnarled into an obnoxious attention-seeking little monster who knows she doesn't fit in but doesn't know why or what to do about it except keep flying that freak flag. In all our childhood photos, Little Jessie had a tragic penchant for a wide-mouthed, misshapen roar rather than a smile. Little Dani is gazing clear-eyed into the camera, absolutely beautiful, often wearing a bunny outfit. I look like a deranged, blond monkey. Is it any wonder Little Chip was like, *"Get me out of here"*?

I grew up desperately wanting Chip to approve of me. When I was in middle school I used to steal his t-shirts. It didn't even matter if he had already worn them. I would dig around in his hamper to find the one I wanted (this was a phase when I really liked baggy clothes), wear it, then sneak it back into the hamper at the end of the day. It wasn't hard to hide that I was wearing his t-shirt because Chip generally avoided looking at me, but sometimes he caught me and it would make him furious. I kept doing it anyway.

As I got older, I deliberately befriended guys Chip's age, desperate to prove to myself that I was likable, substituting the brotherly attention I craved. Later, this translated to an unfortunate penchant for dating boys that lived out of state, and I was always running up the family phone bill. This earned me the nickname "The Expensive Child," a nomenclature I have yet to declaw from my psyche. Whereas Chip's every instinct was to be reasonable, I gravitated toward farther (and more expensive) vistas, putting additional strain on our parents. I tried to compensate by exploiting my talents to get scholarships. But by being ambitious and unconventional, I was a burden; I was a traitor.

Dani and I agree: Growing with us probably sucked. We were obnoxiously dyadic. Chip was the odd man out. Maybe this was in part because our parents didn't force Chip to attend our functions, our choral concerts and plays and athletic games. Maybe they gave him leeway because he was the eldest boy, and they understood what an interminable drag it would be to listen to his sisters' middle-school show choir sing Kirby Shaw songs with accompanying hand choreography. Which maybe led to a missed opportunity to have some common topics to discuss. Such as why on earth did your choir director choose that stupid song, and why on earth did they heap stupid hand choreography on top of it? We could have debated that together. But instead, we did our thing and Chip did his. The silence grew. I suspect this was mostly my fault. I felt responsible for Dani, especially once our mother took on the burden of caring for her elderly parents, but maybe I used that to give Chip the finger. Like, *"See? THIS is what a sibling friendship looks like!"* Or maybe I was shrugging him off, *"Fine, I don't need you to like me because **she** does."* Or maybe my longing for Chip's approval translated to a kind of platonic Come Hither, like, *"Oh hey, I'm over here playing Barbie Prom but just say the word and you and I can wear your t-shirts into the brother-sister sunset."* But that never happened. Dani and I were a unit. And Chip was constantly outside our bond.

So when Chip had two daughters, and they turned out to have a close relationship like Dani and I, we were like, Oh nooooooo! Chip is living through it all over again! A kind of Sister-Club Groundhog Day. But watching Chip's relationship with his wife and daughters has provided an opportunity to see how Chip should be loved and cared for. They are candid, humorous, even when expressing emotionality. I've watched both of his daughters in moments of duress—when the classic father-daughter misfires can easily occur—respond to Chip with robust openness. By being authentic and honest about their feelings, they demonstrated their trust in their safety with him. I have mostly failed to be as brave.

But while Chip's family is clearly the happiest chapter of his life, don't ask him about it because he'd rather be left alone. Like for real. If you try to make small talk, even nice stuff like, "Hey, I hear your family is the happiest chapter of your life," it is highly likely he will raise his eyebrows and then pretend you're not there. Small talk is like a machete to Chip's gas tank. He immediately drains out.

I remember when Chip's wife Emily planned a surprise party for his fortieth birthday. Chip walked around and greeted his colleagues from the high school where he was at the time an assistant principal. I was wide-eyed, jaw gaping—he was so friendly. Clearly well-liked and respected, he made his rounds to each table, bringing everyone to laughter, thanking them for being there. The Chip I grew up with could be sullen, grumpy. I watched him connect with his birthday guests and said, "Excuse me, who is this? And why can't *he* come to family dinner now and then?" He chuckled. He knew what I meant.

When Dani described me as wild flowers and herself as a well-mowed lawn, we asked ourselves: *What does that make Chip?* The answer: A white picket fence. A tall, thick one. With motion sensitive flood lights. Protecting the entire yard from unwanted intruders. Once inside that white picket fence, Chip takes good care and keeps close watch. But it's hard to gain access to the yard.

My first husband never made it.

To be fair, Chip has never warmed to any of our partners. Dani's husband Alan has been in our family for over twenty years and it's possible he's still on shaky ground. It's not that Chip is unkind to Alan. He just ignores him. In the beginning, he ignored him out of a wish he would disappear. Now he ignores him out of respect that Alan is one of the family. Chip cares most about loyalty and responsibility, traits Alan Neff has in profound spades, so I've no doubt Alan has Chip's respect.

In other words, I didn't give it much weight when Chip didn't like the dude I married. I equated Chip's disapproval of my husband with his disapproval of me. Or my perception of his disapproval of me. I never flat out asked him, "Do you disapprove of me?" Maybe I was afraid of the answer. But I've never found it easy to talk to my brother.

Except when my first marriage ended.

Then he was the person I most urgently needed to talk to.

After a sleepless night, I left Dani's house and drove through the crisp morning sunshine to Chip's. Emily was out of town running a marathon, my parents were out of town visiting friends in Florida, and I was grateful for those absences. I didn't know what Chip would say, I just knew it would be the brutal truth. As he saw it. And I desperately wanted to know how he saw it. Maybe he would shame me with my failure. Take satisfaction in seeing me laid low. The deranged, blond monkey was finally going to Eat Shit. I had no idea if I was ruining my life, but I knew of all my family, Chip would be the most critical, the most conservative. He would tell it like he saw it and it was likely to be unbridled and harsh.

I found Chip and his daughters around back. Chip was finishing up a yard project, so Nora and Evie and I played something they called Flower Hospital, which entailed taking tiny sticks and building support around all the flowers in the yard. From clover to clover we went, balancing twig scaffolding from the base of the clover to its pale fragrant top. The metaphor was not lost on me.

He told the girls we needed time alone and they went upstairs to play. I told him everything I could. He listened. And then he began with words I had no idea how desperately I needed to hear: "Jess, I've watched you worry about this for at least five years." He described what he'd observed, the separate paths my husband and I had slowly chosen, that the path I'd have to take to stay in my marriage didn't seem like one that was good for me. As the years would pass and ground would be gained between myself and my divorce, the veracity of this would prove itself tenfold. But Chip had seen it all along. I was facing something I'd tried not to face. I wasn't ruining my life. I was claiming it.

I was shocked. I was relieved. Chip saved my life that day.

But Chip saves a lot of lives every day. Now the head principal of that high school, Chip has stepped into his prime as a leader and educator. Having learned to manage the world's ability to ruin everything by simply *planning for it* is Chip's superpower. His hyper vigilance was perfectly suited for pandemic times, and I know his teachers and administrators have felt lucky and grateful—Chip was always thinking twenty steps ahead, planning everything within an inch of its life, all so that a graduation or a band concert could be possible. Chip's picket fence now includes a high school of students and faculty. Lucky them.

Five years after that morning in Chip's living room, Dani gave me a journal for my birthday. This was a very practical gift as I journal every day and usually need a new one every four months. But this journal was special: Dani had my friends and family write notes of encouragement throughout the journal. So I'd be writing along on some winter morning, turn the page, and there would be a message from someone who loves me. There were so many beautiful sentiments in those pages, and the love and generosity in the gift is absolutely emblematic of Dani. But my favorite missive in the book is from Chip.

He wrote: "You are a great example to my girls. You show them that believing in yourself and working hard pays off. That doesn't mean I want them to run off to NYC but you get the point." That last line is Classic Chip: Sentimentality tempered with a tinge of *Don't feel too good about this*. But because Chip never gives false praise, the compliment went right to my heart.

I had somehow convinced myself that his white picket fence didn't include me. But that day I learned it did. That day the sistering I desperately needed did not come from a sister.

It came from a brother.

THE GATE

Dani

I'm pretty sure my brother likes me more, even though I'm only a little bit sure that he likes me at all. I do think that when lined up beside each other, Chip sees more in common with me than with Jessie. To start, we look like one another. We have a similar build (which is infinitely more attractive on a man than a woman). If you took all my hair, I would look exactly like Chip.

But more than that, we both have a deep love of order, organization. We both like being in charge, not because we are particularly bossy, but because we believe thoroughly in our organizational skills. It is not uncommon for Chip and I to be on the same page about the logic behind what week we go to the beach, or the route we will take somewhere.

He and I have followed similar life paths. We domesticated our lives very quickly. We went to school. We got jobs. We got married. We had kids. The trajectory clear and trustworthy. We both did those things not because it felt like we "should" or because it was what was expected of us. We did those things because it is endemic to who we are. A traditional life is very appealing to us. We are both deeply happy in routine, in stability. We've both eaten the same cereal for breakfast for the last twenty years and we don't feel like we've missed a thing in doing so.

I suspect that because my sister and I are closer in age (two-and-a-half years between us, versus seven years between my brother and me), we simply had more time together, space to become closer. I was also insufferably annoying as a child. If you wanted me to leave a room, I wouldn't. If you wanted to play, I would inevitably tell on you if it didn't go my way. Typical youngest sibling stuff, but truly, a real bummer to be around if you're an oldest sibling. Chip was so much older that he truly had the option of staying away from both of us. For all the ways that Jessie and I are similar (emotions, humor), my brother and I have the same level of similarities. It's just that the similarities that Jessie and I share have a lot to do with how we communicate. Whereas the similarities my brother and I share simply require a head nod, or a well laid out task list. Both valid and true.

Jessie, our wildflower-breezy-creative-honeysuckle, surrounded by a square, well-cut lawn for a sister and a well-maintained wooden fence for a brother. I know that is classic birth order stuff—the middle child as the wild card.

But in our threesome, I've always felt in the middle. Torn. Because Chip and Jessie both represent parts of me that are equally true and important. I feel like the translator. The bridge. The Switzerland. Loyal to both, but disloyal, too. Speaking more clearly the language of my sister and living more closely the life of my brother.

I have become closer with my brother in my adulthood, and I'm so glad for it. We have recently started tiptoeing into the waters of calling one another. It is usually because we have a practical thing to discuss (here is the website to look at our choices, here is the plan for dinner at mom and dad's)—but now, instead of hanging up, we linger on the phone and talk. We talk about work—we are both in charge of large organizations and answer to boards (him as a principal, me as a senior pastor) and so there are real similarities to the stressors and expectations placed on us.

My relationship with my brother first changed when he met his wife, Emily. It was always a question what kind of person my brother would marry. We never really met any of his girlfriends and so had no idea what qualities he found endearing and interesting. Imagine our surprise when Chip married someone... like us. Like Jessie and me.

Emily is creative, loving, funny. She's also tough, loud, and driven. We loved her immediately. As Jessie said so well, in Emily we see how Chip needs to be loved and cared for. She sees Chip—what's underneath a hard exterior—because she is intuitive, but also because he shows her. She also takes no shit—she doesn't suffer his bad moods or gruffness. She is loyal. She is impressive—an award-winning educator and a mind-bogglingly dedicated runner. But best of all, she loves our brother, and she values deeply being taken care of by Chip. She lets Chip provide; she lets him be the fence.

There is a common narrative that in-law relationships have to be contentious, difficult, strained. Emily is proof that's not true. Emily saw our family, she saw Jessie and me, and instead of walling herself off, she thought, "I can be a part of that." And she is; she really is. She's our sister. And she helped us be better sisters to Chip. If Jessie is the wildflowers, I'm the lawn, and Chip is the fence... Emily is the open gate.

UNCONDITIONAL POSITIVE REGARD

Jessie

If I showed up at Dani's door and told her I'd just shot someone, she would probably say the following:

1. Get in the car. You can explain while we hide the body.
2. I'm sure you did your best and they probably deserved it.
3. Considering the circumstances, your skin looks amazing.

Everyone needs this.

Everyone needs someone they run to when shit hits the fan. Someone who radically believes in them. Someone who lets them tell their darkest feelings, be their crappiest self, drop any pretense of being perfect or good. Someone who sees it all and still makes them feel known and loved.

Everyone needs someone who holds them in unconditional positive regard.

Unconditional positive regard asserts that we are innately worthy, and we have everything we need to change and evolve. It was popularized by the psychologist Carl Rogers in the mid-1950s and the idea revolutionized the field of psychology. When a person experiences unconditional faith in their worthiness of love and acceptance, they can then take responsibility for their lives and choices.

If this doesn't describe my relationship with Dani, I don't know what does.

Unconditional positive regard is our theology.

That doesn't mean we ignore our failings. On the contrary, this dynamic creates the robust intimacy ideal for facing them. I know Dani is profoundly loving and caring; I also know she can cut a bitch. She doesn't forgive easily. I also understand *why* she is this way; how important this is for protecting the profound caregiving that directs her way of being in the world. But that's the point: Unconditional positive regard means understanding why someone is the way they are, and believing in the innate goodness of it.

Isn't that what God's love is supposed to be? I'm no expert, but I have been hanging out with Dani since 1981, so from that I can make an educated guess:

God's love is a verb. It's dropping off a casserole when someone loses a loved one. Or gives birth to a loved one. It's sitting next to someone when their husband has a stroke and it is not clear when and if he will ever be himself again. God's love is creating a program for filling backpacks with food for kids who are growing up with food insecurity to take home to their families. God's love is creating a space for women to connect with themselves and each other and evaluate how they're really doing and what they need and how to be a spiritual woman *and* a modern woman. God's love is biting your tongue in the pulpit to protect the political diversity you have in your congregation so that no one feels alienated and everyone somehow is brought to the heart space, the space to feel the hurt of our violent world and to heal. God's love is sending a poem at seven o'clock in the morning because it reminds you of your sister's struggle to feel worthy of the new happiness after her divorce. God's love is remembering the anniversary of someone's death and reaching out to the family. Or the date of someone's surgery and visiting them in the hospital. God's love is noticing that someone seemed sad for the third week in a row and touching their arm and asking how they're doing in the greeting line.

You get it.

Sometimes when I tell people my sister is a pastor, I feel them cock their head and say, "Huh." I feel them think of

Fox News and the Christian Right. I feel them associate her with words like bigoted, simple, goody-goody. I catch myself compensating by saying things like, "My sister is a pastor. But like, a really really rad one; a really liberal, progressive one. And super cool. She cusses more than me. And burps. Really loudly. And has road rage. And dances like a hussy." (All of which is very true.) And then I slump a little bit. I hate myself a little bit. Because that's their problem if they don't know that just because the extreme rightwing Christian movement is a vocal minority that screams loudly into microphones outside Planned Parenthoods and school boards, it doesn't mean every Christian is an asshole. I want to say to them that if there are any redeeming traits they see in me, they could magnify it thirty times and get *close* to my sister. She's top shelf. She's classy AF. She's funny and irreverent. She dances like the hoochiest music video you can imagine and she drinks Coca-Cola like a mofo. She's not perfect. But she's *really, really great*.

Everyone needs someone who is Team You. All the way.

As I type this, Dani is in front of me. She came to France (!) and we are working on the book. She is staring at our wall full of notes and outlines, and she is doing a little humpy dance and making up new lyrics to a song from the nineties.

Now she's pointing and flexing her foot like she did when she was eight.

Now she's contemplating her chin (or *chins*, she would say).

Now she's doing the little humpy dance again and the lyrics are about getting old. She's the best.

Forever and ever.

Amen.

I DIDN'T TELL HER

Dani

The first time I met Josh, he told me that he didn't believe in God. I don't mean that this came up after an awkward family dinner and a few glasses of wine. No, I mean that these were the actual first words out of his mouth.

"Dani! Hi! So... you're uh... gonna be a minister? Wow. Yeah. I don't believe in God."

Truth is, I honestly don't care if someone believes in God. I mean, I care because I think God is the best, but it has no bearing on whether or not I'll love you or want to talk to you or think you're interesting. So, it was not that

Jessie's new boyfriend (later husband) was an atheist that bothered me. It was that in the inaugural sentences in our relationship, Josh chose to place us in presumed opposition to one another.

I mean, it really takes something to begin a conversation, begin a relationship, by taking a verbal poop on someone's life devotion.

"Oh, you're a doctor?...I think antibiotics are a sham."

"Oh, you're a social worker?...I think poor people are lazy."

"Oh, you're a teacher?...I think the school system is a waste of tax dollars."

You get it.

Of course, I don't think Josh did that intentionally. I don't think he entered the conversation suspicious of me or wanting to test me, or even throw shade. And yet somehow, in our first moments of conversation, he found a way to create a separation, a barrier. It took me a long time—years even—of knowing Josh to understand that maybe this is how he is in relationship to everyone. That perhaps he defined himself, even his most intimate relationships, not in shared experience, but in what separates.

Josh was boisterous, gregarious, funny, joyful, energetic, and always placed himself as the other. In opposition to. In contrast to. Even when you agreed, you somehow always found yourself feeling alone. In his agreement, he only ever gave enough to let you feel like there was a small thread that for this one conversation could tie you—but only for today.

In Jessie, Josh had someone who knew how to build a relationship on a thread. Someone who could make a rope out of that thread, could weave a blanket out of that thread. Because Jessie is one of those people who finds *everyone* interesting. One of Jessie's superpowers is finding something to love in everyone. And when she finds that thing, she can build on it. She can build whole kingdoms around what is loveable in you. Thank God. Because I can be a wretched crone sometimes, and my sister thinks that's a really delightful quality in me. She loves it when I'm spicy and sarcastic and biting. When I am the most jagged version of myself, when I am an actual cactus plant of aggression, my sister finds where she can hug me.

And Josh wasn't a cactus, he had many good qualities, but he was also selfish, and he saw that goodness in Jessie, that desire to connect and make pathways and loved her for it. I think he loved that probably for one of the first times in his life he could place himself in opposition to someone and still feel connected to them.

It's probably not fair for me to say all this, a postmortem dissection eight years after their divorce. But I'm the sister, so I'm allowed to because witnessing the divorce clicked it all into place. The divorce clicked into place the previous decade that I spent wondering why I just couldn't connect with Josh, couldn't understand Josh—maybe even didn't *like* Josh. Because no matter how many visits and conversations, I think I didn't trust Josh to take care of my sister.

And I never told her. Jessie is the person in this world that I am most honest with. I don't hide myself from Jessie and yet I didn't tell her this. No one in our family really did. The only one who came close was our brother, who didn't so much tell her, but rather nurtured a seething resentment for Josh that was palpable every time they shared a room. Everyone else, we didn't even let ourselves entertain being anything other than one hundred percent supportive of Josh, or Jessie and Josh.

Who would it have served? What good could it have done to tell her, "I see that you love him, but I don't trust him"? I would either alienate myself from her or alienate her from her spouse. Neither of those seemed like good options and I couldn't conceive of any other outcomes. I don't know that I understood all this with such clarity anyway. It's the kind of realization that comes in retrospect. Like after a thousand paper cuts, you realize you've got a wound. You realize that you maybe should have stopped trying to turn the page that way. In the moment, one cut, one turn of the page doesn't feel like such a big deal, but over time you see the cost of those small concessions. Relationships *require* self-sacrifice, compromise. Who was I to tell Jessie that she was sacrificing too much or compromising to her detriment?

Mostly, I thought I was just being a jerk. I thought I was the jerk who didn't want another person to love her as much as I did. I thought I was a jerk who didn't believe another person *could* love her as well as I could. And I'm an Enneagram 2, so maybe it was also a little bit that I wasn't sure where I would fit in or stand in her life if I wasn't the person she knew loved her more than anyone.

On the night that her marriage broke in half they each went into the conversation the way they approached everything. Jessie went into the conversation with full commitment to connection. He went into the conversation with full commitment to opposition. And I find the hubris in his position breathtaking but not entirely surprising.

When I picked her up on the actual side of the road (I will never forgive him for that), she was barely standing. She was shell-shocked and exhausted and bereft. I have this picture of her in the days following that breaking, and she is lying in front of our fireplace. She's curled up on the floor like a cat. She has a thick sweater on and maybe even a blanket covering her. She's curled up so close to the fire, I'm not sure how the skin didn't melt off her face. I think she felt so profoundly alone that she was physically cold. I was desperately trying to figure out how I was going to crawl into the womb of that grief and just hold her in it. I was desperately trying to figure out how I could become the womb itself.

But that's not how people can go through these things, or at least it's not how Jessie could. She wanted no protection from the relentless onslaught of shame, grief, anger, sadness that divorce brought to her. She let me walk beside her. She let me be a person she called in the middle of the night. But there was no shielding her from it. The only way past it was through it, and I admire how much she yielded herself to going through it. I admire the constant mirror she held up to herself and I hated that I knew Josh wasn't holding up any such mirror to himself. I hated that he always let *her* find the fault lines, to be the antagonist, the fool, the person who learns the lesson. I hated that after years of her compromise and compassion, he had none to show.

As much as possible, I tried to sometimes take the mirror and hold it for her instead, as though somehow the person holding the mirror could imbue what *they* see. When Jessie held her mirror, I think she saw failure and selfishness and brokenness. When I held the mirror, I hope she saw what I did—bravery, strength, truth, growth.

A wise colleague told me once that "people tell themselves the story they need to hear in order to leave." One of the things she said a lot during that time was, "It helps when you remind me." She needed to be reminded that the story she was telling in the leaving was true. She needed to be reminded that the story she was telling about who she was becoming was a story worth writing, and it was a story that wasn't going to stop in this terrible moment, and it was a story that though it would take up a giant chapter, would most definitely not be the defining one. She needed to be reminded that whatever story Josh was telling himself in the leaving, whatever was true for him, didn't have to be true for her, it didn't have to be her story. Her story could be written differently.

What I saw in the months after Jessie's divorce was that she was finding her protagonist, she was discovering which version of herself was going to lead her life. The divorce was devastating, but it was also a moment when Jessie was claiming what she wanted. She was casting a vision that was unabashedly ambitious. She was gulping in the fresh air of manifest destiny.

At the same time, she was ashamed of that. In our family of origin, we were raised to be loyal. We were expected to be gentle. We were raised to have intense integrity and never, ever quit. We were raised to be exceptional. In that family system and narrative, there was no room for marriage failure, no room for divorce. Despite this deep training, my parents were instantly and unequivocally supportive of my sister throughout this terrible season.

In this season where Jessie began claiming the deep ambition and truth within herself, she wasn't just leaving her marriage. She was leaving, to some degree, the deeply codified ethic of our family. What would it mean to live this part of her life for herself alone? To follow the compass that was guiding her to place her deepest wants at the center? To not just excel for the sake of something or someone else, but to move intentionally toward that actualization for herself? Terrifying.

Terrifying, but watching it was breathtaking. That she let me walk beside her, let me hold the mirror for her, let me remind her she was still good—was a privilege.

It strikes me that this is what we do in ministry—we try to be the mirror that reflects to people what God sees. Where people look at themselves and are ashamed, we try to show them grace. Where people see brokenness, we try to show them what God can do with broken things. Where people look at themselves and see whatever terrible thing, we try to reflect that God sees goodness and love. In a life of faith, we try to break ourselves of the habit of thinking the worst of ourselves and each other—and replace it with the truth of what God sees. Where we might see ourselves only as the antagonist, in the eyes of God, we are protagonists, we are loved for the story we are writing.

The path of Jessie's healing after the divorce was to help her tell her story, or what I would say is God's story, versus the story that others have about us. It was painful and excruciatingly slow, but the divorce was how Jessie broke the habit of giving herself away so that someone else could feel like something or someone. The divorce was when Jessie stopped letting others use her—her failures, her successes, her goodness—to build themselves up and instead looked in the mirror and saw who she really was: powerful and good. Strong and courageous. Herself.

DIVORCE IS

Jessie

Divorce is a vat of shame.
Divorce is a D- on one of the most important tests of life.
Divorce is public failure.
With fifty percent of marriages, divorce is cliché.

Divorce is admission. It says, I suck. My spouse sucked. I sucked and I gave up. It reveals on some level you've been lying. To yourself, to your friends. And with every person you encounter, you sense that they are holding an invisible stone. They turn it over and over in their palm, seductively cupping its smooth, cool hardness. Sometimes they are jealous. Sometimes they are incensed. Sometimes they are afraid. In all cases they are looking at you and debating whether to raise their arm... and throw.

Divorce is expressionism. It's a painting by Cézanne. The closer you look, the blurrier the lines; the more you cannot tell where one thing stops and another starts. Her skirt brushes into the sky, which brushes into the mountain, which brushes into his hair. You cannot tell where your ex ends and you begin. You cannot describe his cheapness, or his issues with work, without smudging into your own insecurity about your worth, your own ability to earn, your own dependence on work for your identity. You cannot remember how loving he could be without bumping into your own longing for his love and failure to love him the way he needed.

I always found it difficult to say bad things about my ex. I still struggle to say bad things about him, even with all that fucking therapy. I do say them now, but it still hurts. Because I loved him and I believed in him. Even if it's easier now to say the things about my ex that I found untenable, I still want to take his hand and apologize for saying them. For seeing them at all. For finally accepting they were true. And for releasing myself of responsibility for them. If Dani has taught me that to love someone is to be their mirror, and to hold up for them the most loving, truthful, faithful reflection of who they are, but also who they are aspiring to be—to be the archive for the life behind them that made them wherever they are on that journey currently—I know my ability to be that kind of mirror for my ex slowly eroded away.

Divorce is exposure. Because all marriages are a cult of two. And all marriages are secretive. So divorce is a relief because you can finally tell your secrets. You can admit how you really felt. You can stop pretending you're a good person. The loving partner you were desperately trying to be. You can let it all drop. When you talk to other people about your divorce, you are inevitably trafficking in *their* divorce. Their marriage. Whatever contracts, compromises, secrets they have made. So when you talk about your divorce, proceed gently. And zip up your lavender shield. The terrain is war torn and hard won.

But despite all these things, and in fact *because of them* ...

Divorce is a gift.

I will forever be grateful for divorce as the moment that I understood you can make decisions for your life, based on what you think you want and need. And if you eventually realize those decisions were *wrong*, you can change your mind; you can make different decisions. Divorce teaches you that your decisions are just that—decisions. And they are yours.

Divorce was the moment I claimed my own life. The sovereignty of my own life. Especially when I realized I didn't actually need reasons. This was terrifying. Especially since that is exactly what everyone asks when you say you're getting divorced: Why? What happened? As if you yourself have the answer. As if you yourself won't spend the rest of your life grappling to understand that very thing. I did have reasons. So did he. But in the end, I arrived at the striking truth that the only reason I really needed was because I wanted to go. I knew I should go. My own compass was enough.

I am grateful to the friends who tried to hold us both during that process. Because divorce is (inevitably) a competition. For narrative validity. For who is more right, or more wronged. For who is doing better now. In this sense, divorce is ugly. Very ugly. But what a *relief*. In a marriage where I'd tried to keep it nice, drowning in the many hard things I was seeing and trying to say kindly, feeling powerless to be trusted, to be heard, it was such a relief to just let it go. Let the curtain drop. Hello, world. I'd like to introduce you to Crappy Me. Here I am. Thank God.

And suddenly all that fuel I was burning, voraciously trying to keep it up—trying to keep *him* up—trying to hang back enough to keep him close and yet still somehow keep my own forward movement going... It was like the ropes snapped and broke and all that energy boomeranged back into my own body, my own life. I was *coursing* with power. It was thrilling. Terrifying. I was grieving. But if I'm honest, I was trying *really hard* to grieve. Because most of my being was *thrumming* with freedom. I felt overwhelmed. I felt alight. I felt guilty. I felt worried about him. I felt euphoric. I felt free. I felt *right*.

There was so much good learning en route to that moment. Much of which I owe my ex. He was my partner in that learning. My cheerleader. My fellow journeyer. And my antagonist. And I am grateful to him.

But the biggest gift of my divorce was discovering I am in contact with a presence inside myself. Almost like an uber me. Like a Jessie that is the dimension of the sky. And as lit. But inside me. Watching. Waiting. And somehow, during the early spring of 2014, she pierced through. It took ten years of individual (and group) therapy, establishing myself as a writer, and crossing the Atlantic Ocean for a solo trip, but she breached the thick flooring of my marriage, my life, and *spoke*. And I *heard her*. And what she told me was uncompromising. It was impossible. But it was the truth.

And in that way, divorce is scorched earth. It is standing in the center of the ashes and inhaling a night full of stars.

It is sacred.

It is courage.

It is new beginning.

Divorce is victory.

MY OVARIES DON'T WORK

Dani

When Alan and I were trying to get pregnant with our third child, it took a while. We had settled into a mantra of "it will happen." I tried not to get too worked up about month after month of getting my period, the disappointing familiarity of cramps when you hoped there would be none. My doctor kept reminding me that I was older (I was thirty-seven) and so perhaps it would simply take more time than the previous two pregnancies (where I practically just looked at Alan and became pregnant). In truth, what I went through doesn't fit the medical description of infertility (a year of trying to get pregnant with no success). It was more like eight months. But having a third child was not a dream I was ready to let go of.

It was an evening the first week of March in 2018 when I came home and took a pregnancy test.

Just the night before, Alan and I had sat down together and agreed it was time to accept that we would have two lovely children and be content. We made a little inventory of the plans we had now that the boys were getting older. More traveling. Professional goals. Personal commitments. Then the next day there it was, those two lines amidst a small panel of white. The eggo is prego. Alan's response, "Holy Shit. Well. Okay then."

What I know now is that that little Gracie egg was probably the last good one in the cache. And with a will that is so very evident in her pint-sized body now, she manifested herself into existence.

They call it a geriatric pregnancy when you get pregnant past the age of thirty-five. When they are feeling generous, they say you are of "advanced maternal age." All fancy ways of saying, "You are old."

I am *not* old. I can still sing along with half the songs on the top twenty countdown. I am the youngest sibling. I'm on TikTok for shit's sake. I am not of advanced maternal age.

I had one, maybe two periods after Grace was born. Then nothing. I was thirty-eight. The universal refrain was that my periods would normalize after Grace was done breastfeeding. Then it was after my hormones normalized. Then it was just "give it time." A full year later—nothing. Nada. Not a drop. Not a cramp.

You know what's worse than the title, "geriatric pregnancy"? Premature Ovarian Failure. Primary Ovarian Insufficiency. Otherwise known as Premature Menopause; aka, your ovaries are now fossils; aka, your uterus is now a canyon; aka, your hormones are laughing at you. Aka, the red sea has parted ways from you.

I know these are medical terms. I know they say nothing about who I am or who loves me or my worth, but do they have to be so . . . *descriptive*? So utterly focused on accuracy? So telling of what is now over in my life?

When my sister put the faux-bloody pad on my pillow when I was nine, none of us were thinking, "You've only got twenty-six years of monthly bleeding. The window of which said bleeding will actually be useful will be frighteningly small. And then it will be done. Gone. No more."

Even though a year of amenorrhea had me knowing that I was in menopause, when the actual diagnosis came, I was gutted. The finality of it a sharp jab where I least expected it.

Part of that heartache was because it meant the end of something—the end of being able to have biological children. But truthfully, I didn't want more children. I had three and hit the lottery with each of them.

No, I think I was gutted because I had not realized how fully I had bought into youth or beauty or fertility being an indicator of my value. I had no idea, until this diagnosis, that I had firmly and deeply been indoctrinated into the church of ageism.

How deeply ashamed I felt at the realization.

Jessie is one of the few people I talk to about aging. We are both in professions where people *see* you. Where you are on display. In ministry, there is an impossible standard where you must be old enough not to be naive or inexperienced or immature—but you shouldn't look *too* old because we need you to "attract the young families." God help you if you are a woman because in addition to those charming expectations, you must also navigate that your voice must not be too high, your demeanor must be soft and warm, but not weak; you must be confident and poised, but not cocky or bossy. Impossible.

In Jessie's profession you can age, but not physically. There can be no wrinkles. There can be no gray hair. And Lord Jesus you absolutely, positively, most definitely cannot have back fat. Or cellulite. Or hair anywhere other than your head. But can you please have a butt? A proportionate one that people want to grab but otherwise won't be noticeably big? Also, be charming. Be persistent but not annoying. Be successful but humble. Make it big, but don't forget to be nice!

What. A. Prison.

What an oppressive, maniacal, sadistic, patronizing heap of lies.

And I bought every single one of them. For myself. I clothed myself in them daily. I smeared them on my face in creams and concealers. I shoved them into wedge heels and blazers. I spritzed it on in mists of perfume. And I did it with a smile that was white with perfectly straight teeth.

And then I stopped bleeding at age thirty-eight, a full decade and a half before most of my peers will, and there was not a thing I could do to correct that. I couldn't serum my way out of it. I couldn't Spanx my way through it.

You are dried up, Neff. Deal with it.

When I told my sister that my ovaries had given up the ghost, she said, "I know this feels big right now, but this is not a thing. This doesn't have to be a thing." She has said other compassionate, empathic, important things but this is the one that sticks with me. I was so angry when she said it because her ovaries are still working to this day (and she's *older than me*), but I held on to it, because I knew she was right. I knew she was the voice I should listen to, the tape I should keep playing.

I'm forty-one now. I don't give a shit that I don't have my period. Honestly, it's kind of great. I literally never have that awful moment when I think, "Is my tampon full?" I never worry that I will be out on a hike and suddenly bleeding. I never worry about what time it is in my cycle. Whatever. It's dried-up-ovary-o'clock. No matter what, it's the perfect time to do whatever the hell I want.

And you know what? I still want to put on makeup and wear some heels and hold my own power. I still want to be soft and loving and kick some ass. I still want to be a person in the world. Who cares if I'm bleeding? But I do all those things now for a different reason. I do them for me. I thought I did them for me before. I didn't—at least not deep down. Now, I do.

Advanced Maternal Age. Primary Ovarian Insufficiency.
How about Advanced Primary Bad-Ass?
That's more like it.

PART THREE

benedictions

SENSE OF PLACE

~ ❁ ~

Jessie

It is summer in the little village of Saint Bauzille de Putois, and the evening is lavender colored. The last of the day's kayaks have long finished their clamor down the river that wends next to the village, the whoops and whoahs of the day's outdoors-ing absorbed by the water and the rocks. Large trout flash a fin above the surface. Blue heron sit in the trees. In a few hours, wild boars will trot out of the forest for the night's foraging. The Milky Way will shimmer.

This is where I live now.

I watch this lush evening from our terrace. Above my head, swallows dive for insects. The last of the light casts a blue glow on the limestone cliffs that rise up behind the river, crowned with the thorny garrigue of southern France: spiny broom and rosemary, wild thyme and stunted holly oaks.

Our home is the center unit in a converted old silk factory. I have an office downstairs where I write and do meetings every day. Benoît, a neuroscientist, has an office upstairs where he works (when not in the lab in Montpellier). While I can easily list many things that are hard about living in a foreign country—the stress before the simplest of tasks, like going to the pharmacy, putting gas in the car, turning onto a road that cannot possibly be a two-way street but is—when people here ask if it was hard to go from Brooklyn, New York, to such a small place, I say no, because I am from a small place.

Saint Bauzille de Putois and Waynesboro have many commonalities: after bedtime it's so quiet you can walk down the middle of the street. There are Those Who Have Been Here Forever, and they resent Those Who Are from Somewhere Else. There are Those Who Wish to Make It More Than It Is, and there are Those Who Want to Keep It What It Was. It has a pride in its own beauty, alongside a sheepish shame about its smallness. It has kindness and loneliness, jealousy and generosity.

This morning Benoît and I walked to the market, a courageous initiative in Saint Bauzille by Those Who Wish to Make It More Than It Is. At first many locals were suspicious, but now they too come to the market. Sometimes we see a neighbor and spontaneously join them for a glass of wine (yes, before noon). We set down our totes of vegetables and pull out pastries and olive bread and share with the table. We chat about the weather, how work is going, the way real estate is changing.

I don't speak French very well, but I have found a way to share who I am with the people who live here. I use a lot of hand gestures. (A lot.) I use my big American smile. I use my comedic timing. I use my ability to stay vulnerable, buttressed by my stubborn insistence on poise. More and more I can patch together what people are saying. I try to be honest when I don't understand, but it's hard. Benoît has gotten very good at leaning close and filling me in now and then. More and more people are comfortable trying their English with me, and this is incredibly kind. I try to be brave and just stab away at what I want to say. We manage. Occasionally I am crestfallen, consumed with a humiliating ache that what has always been my friend, my comfort with words, is not with me now. I try to have faith I will get there.

I feel so lucky it's almost painful. I get to do the work that I love, and I get to live in a beautiful place. Every day I walk the hills and country lanes around our village. Roads so narrow you can only think of the Middle Ages. I cut through pastures thick with the musk of local sheep, dotted with miniature wild orchids the size of my pinky nail. I smile and say "Bonjour" to the people who walk their dogs. All the while I think about whatever I am working on—that plot point at the end of the teaser, the emotional confession that propels act four. This daily routine is my productive way to prepare for the day's writing, or to refresh it.

In Brooklyn, I wrote on my couch. And on the subway. And between jobs. All while desperate to find money to pay my bills. Don't get me wrong; I am proud of that time. I did it. I made it. I can live the life I have now because of the hustle I hustled then.

I still hustle, but there are more comforts. My writing now has an office. It has an entire cork wall on which to pin the images and outlines. It has an enormous whiteboard on which to track notes and ideas. It has a terrace on which to sit and breathe. It has a sunset and a river beside which bask ancient mysteries.

As a child I remember pretending that my bedroom was my own apartment. I loved the idea of living alone someday. I padded down to the kitchen and rummaged through drawers until I found a metal mixing bowl. I filled it with water and set it on the little table in front of my bedroom window and pretended it was my sink. I had a candle in the shape of a butterfly and I lit it. At one point the flame seemed a little high, so I poured water on it. The flame suddenly scorched upwards, dangerously licking the thin white window curtains, then went out. I padded back downstairs to my parents in the dining room and informed them of the situation: I had almost lit the curtains on fire, but everything was fine now.

Around that same age, Dani and I would take over the TV room upstairs to make a fort. We'd remove all the cushions from the couch and prop them against each other to make the walls, and then use sheets and blankets to be the roof. We'd go in and out of our homemade house. Or we would play Store. Whenever we did this one of us in the scenario was always named "Nitzen." This name stuck; as we got older we referred to someone who was annoying as a "Nitz." If something was annoying it was "Nitz-y." If you would have told us that we would someday sit in my house in the south of France eating Stinky Butthole Cheese, we would have been speechless. We would have deflected our discomfort by making awkward jokes, surely using some iteration of the word Nitz.

My first apartment in Brooklyn was on Dean Street in beautiful tree-lined Cobble Hill. Josh and I moved to this brownstone top-floor during the fourth year of our relationship. You could see tree tops out every window; the bedroom looked down into the brownstone backyards; the living room had a skylight. Unfortunately, it also had a stained thirty-year-old white carpet, so no matter how many times I rented the cumbersome Carpet Doctor from the local grocery store and devoted my whole day to the task, it still looked dirty and old.

The second apartment we lived in was smaller and cheaper, a junior one-bedroom just a few blocks away on Smith Street. We only lived in it together for a few weeks or months at a time, as the two of us shuttled between various regional theater jobs. But once the marriage disintegrated, I knew I would stay. It had high tin ceilings painted white and a rich brick wall that ran the entire length of the apartment. The windows looked out onto a weird little backyard that sat overgrown and unused. I could hear the life of my neighbors on all sides, particularly the thuds of the family that lived above. I'd wake in the night to the sound of babies crying, or a neighbor coming home from a night out. But the morning light was beautiful and I would sit on my couch and journal, my coffee perched on the side table. Living alone suited me. That's an understatement. Living alone was *heavenly*. I loved that apartment because it was mine. I bought cheap Ikea furniture and covered it with expensive Brooklyn pillows. I loved that every corner of the space was purposed for my work and my comfort. I taught many writing classes there, arranging my chairs around the coffee table, setting out wine and cheese and crackers and grapes and kale salad. Even if the cockroaches were tenacious and I'd have given my left hand for a dishwasher, I would have said the same thing: I feel so lucky it's almost painful. I get to do the work that I love, and I get to live in a beautiful place.

I've always thought of where I live as less about the place itself, and more about what it enables me to do.

I moved to Boston because it enabled me to get my bachelor's in fine arts.

I moved to New York because it enabled me to pursue a life in the theater.

Seventeen years later I moved to France because it enabled me to be with my partner when the pandemic came and the world broke open.

When I write on a television show I live in Los Angeles. Palm trees like dinosaurs jut onto the dirt trails of Griffith Park. The air smells of honeysuckle and car exhaust. Bougainvillea the height of buildings and the color of fuchsia festoons the sidewalk above a row of tent houses. People laugh and share appetizers in beautifully gardened outdoor restaurants. Huge crows and hawks swoop overhead. In the thick brush and hills nearby, coyotes trot with hungry eyes and happy tails.

Regional theater productions have stationed me all over the country—short stints in Chicago, DC, Louisville, Cleveland, Minneapolis, Denver, San Francisco. But no matter where I live, some things stay the same: Every day I drink coffee and journal, I find a way to pleasantly exercise, and I talk to Dani.

Everywhere I live, Dani comes to visit. During these highly anticipated periods of concentrated togetherness, we try to cram it all in: we gorge on local cuisine and binge watch our favorite shows; we shop and go to the movies; we fall asleep talking.

France has been no exception, but it has expanded our vocabulary. Now we tour a nearby cave tattooed with prehistoric art. We gape at an aqueduct built by the Romans. Then we lounge on the terrace and cackle, swatting mosquitos as the sun sets. We devour copious amounts of baguette and stinky cheese. I had no idea Dani loves French cheese! There are many food habits on which we differ: she loves Coke, I love wine; she hates olives, I hate meat. But we share a passion for what we lovingly call Stinky Butthole Cheese. The stinkier and butthole-ier, the better.

When a visit to France nears its end, I get depressed. She does too. It finishes with us hugging in the middle of the tiny Montpellier airport, openly weeping. This is the moment it hits me: we live really far apart. I know we'll talk on the phone the next day. We'll see each other at Christmas. But in this moment I have to send her through security and I have no way of making sure she is okay—that she makes her connection, finds food she likes, navigates all the French, gets sleep on the long flight. It's unbearable.

Who knows where else I may live? I know I will always journal in the morning with my coffee. I will plan my work for the day (and my corresponding walk). And I will call Dani.

TRUST IN THE WORLD

Dani

My parents don't give parenting advice. Thank God. They offer encouragement and if asked, will tell you what they think, but they do not offer unsolicited direction. I think that's because they know there is no one right way to live and everyone is doing the best they can. They know the best way to offer support is in words of encouragement or in concrete gestures of support—a well-timed check just before rent is due, an offer to take the kids for the weekend when they notice you're run down, a load of laundry, a package of cookies in the mail. They have honed the art of how to be present and available to the people they love without being omnipresent, without being overbearing.

I am now a mother and am already learning how difficult it is to be this kind of parent. The kind that provides a frame of love and care and expectation for your child, without inserting yourself into their lives. The kind of parent that nurtures the unique qualities of my child without crafting them in my own image. It is hard, and it involves a tremendous amount of trust. Trust in the home life you've built for them and trust in the world you send them into.

When I think about it, it takes my breath away. Every day, Sam and Liam walk themselves to the bus and get on it, a stranger driving them to a building where they will spend the entire day. Gracie skips into the church building that houses her preschool and eats food prepared by someone else; she gets hugs and encouragement from someone other than me. I have to trust that others will care for them in my stead. I have to trust that the teachers will notice when they are frustrated or hurting. I have to trust that the coaches or band directors will see the heart of my children and love them. I have to trust that they will look out for their interests and sacrifice, if necessary, for the safety of my child (and others). I also have to trust that what I give my child—in love, compassion, empathy, stability—is enough to sustain and guide them when any of those systems fail, when any of that trust is breached.

Because that's the other part about parenting. You send them into the world, trusting that others will care for your children, and knowing that at some point that trust will be broken. You know, without a doubt, that carefully built systems are still imperfect and your child will be hurt. You simply pray it is not too traumatic.

My parents say that when we finally all launched into the world (in their case it was when each of us moved away to go to college), they did not feel sad. Did they miss us? Sure. But they mostly felt that our leaving was the goal. Their care and influence over us would of course continue, but the goal was always to raise confident, resilient children who risked being in the world to build their own lives. I know it is their deepest joy that we all did that. We've built our lives, and because of the way they raised us and the freedom they gave us, we have built lives that are still deeply connected to theirs.

It's easy to frame this idea in reference to parenting and children, but the truth is, we do this with all the people that we love. We leave the ones we love in the care of other people. We do this because we cannot be all things to those we love and it would be selfish and misguided to think we could.

Though Jessie and I have always been close, we have always had to leave each other in the care of other people.

In roommates, in other friends, in friends that become like sisters, in elders and mentors, and most certainly in our partners. Are we a constant presence in each other's lives? Absolutely. But if I died today, I know Jessie has a network of people who sister her, who partner with her, who hold her in unconditional positive regard, and none more so than Benoît.

Jessie is in a white dress with colorful flowers on it. She has flowers in her hair and a bouquet in her hands. They're beaming at each other—Benoît and Jessie. Two local friends stand by as witnesses. We're in a government building in France and I can understand maybe one in ten words they are saying because the entire thing is in French, and the officiant (some kind of public official) has about as much stage presence as a slug, but I'm sobbing anyway.

I helped her pick out that dress—but I didn't. I'm there—but I'm not. Because all of this is happening in France, and I'm in my bed in Pennsylvania and I'm watching her wedding on Marco Polo.

The ceremony ends. I shut off my phone and get back under the covers and hug Alan and go back to sleep. It's four o'clock in the morning local time (ten o'clock in the morning French time). My sister got married, and I wasn't physically there—but I felt like I was in the room.

It's a story of twists and turns about how we got to this day and how none of Jessie's family was there. It's complicated but it can all be boiled down to one word: COVID.

The truth is that none of us needed Jessie to wait a single minute more to marry Benoît and I know she felt that support.

After Jessie's divorce, it felt like a daily exercise in trusting her care to other people in the world, because I couldn't be with her every day. It was most difficult then to be apart from her, but also probably good—because it was then that I was most at risk of smothering her. I had to keep reminding myself to be present, but not oppressive; to provide a holding space but not a cage of comfort; to be encouraging but also leave space for grief. I had to trust that there were other people in her life holding the mirror, too. Showing her how good and special and worthy she was.

And of course, people did.

And through that time, we watched her sense of purpose and place in the world deepen and take root. We watched her flourish and thrive in every aspect of her life. She was traveling, writing, experiencing more and more recognition in her creative pursuits. And the person who lived into that best with her was Benoît—someone who was her equal and trusted companion.

Benoît is a neuroscientist, an entrepreneur, and a professor. He is interesting, he is accomplished, he is kind and generous. Their life together is centered in France where they share a home, though Jessie travels and works in the States many months throughout the year and often he is with her. The flexibility and buoyancy of their relationship allows for the complicated careers that each of them holds. I can see that when they make decisions about how they will navigate a job that Jessie has gotten, or a grant for research that Benoît secured, they do it with their partnership as the thing that all these other things orbit around. It's the strength of that partnership that enables them to encourage one another in their professional pursuits and ultimately support one another's aspirations.

I love Benoît because Jessie does—and honestly, that's enough. But I also love him because I can see that Jessie is the most self-possessed, assured, grounded, fulfilled that she has ever been—not because of him, but because he is unafraid of her light, her flourishing. Her previous experiences led her to this renaissance, but I feel like Benoît is one reason that she feels she can trust that this is a sustainable change, a change that is foundational and trustworthy… that she can trust that she deserves this life she has worked so hard for.

As caretakers, as people who love others, there is nothing more satisfying than trusting the world to receive your beloved... and finding that they do.

BRINGING LIAM TO A DEATHBED

Dani

I'm sitting on the radiator in the dining room. We're in the new house, which is new to us but is actually one hundred years old. There is a big window that frames the view from the radiator down a slope. I'm two years old and I'm watching bulldozers push around dirt. The dirt, reddish brown and crumbly, is being flattened and packed down, preparing for a row of condominiums that will be built. My grandmother is behind me in her amigo (electric scooter) explaining what they are doing, perhaps because I was scared of them. I didn't like loud, industrial things. (Don't even get me started on the car wash).

The scene is one that is common in families—a grandparent and a grandchild enjoying a moment together. What makes this scene unique is that we had moved into that house for the expressed purpose of my grandparents moving in with us. The reasons for them moving in with us are varied and complicated, but the primary reason was that both of them were in declining health (one with multiple sclerosis and one with Parkinson's disease). Though both my Nan and Gramps were infirm, they were both mentally and emotionally fit. They were my primary caretakers during the day when my parents were at work.

I shared a birthday with my Nan. My mom loves to tell the story of calling my Nan on her birthday (June 18) and saying to her, "I think you'll love your birthday present—it's a baby girl!" And my Nan screaming and dropping the phone in her excitement. My Grampy and I shared a special relationship. He took me to the diner to get cinnamon Danishes slathered in butter. He delivered me to preschool every day. But my Nan and I, we were constantly together when I was young. She played games with me, she let me do her hair and play beauty salon (and then paid me *real* money!). She would glide into the kitchen on her scooter and give me a cooking lesson on how to make a spice cake or her favorite drink (orange and cranberry juice mixed together). She was the one who taught me that when you called someone's house, you had to say, "Hello Mrs. Weller, may I please speak to Elizabeth?"

She also taught me about holding dignity when disease would seem to take it away. She was gracious in the way she received the care of others. When I look back, I imagine how much it must have humiliated her to absolutely, totally, and completely need someone to lift her on and off the toilet. I imagine how frustrating it must have been to be at the mercy of everyone else's schedules, or how infuriating it must have been when people mistook her disability for a lack of intellect or hearing or ability to speak for herself. Yet my Nan bore these indignities with patience, humor, and love. She did not raise or voice or exhibit frustration at others, but neither did she shrink from correcting misassumptions or making clear her own needs and wants. She was remarkable in this way. There is a scripture passage (Paul's words in 2 Corinthians) that talks about how power is made perfect in weakness. Brené Brown New Aged it up a little bit and said that there is strength in vulnerability. In my Nan, this was unequivocally true. She exemplified the scripture, "Therefore, I'm all right with weaknesses… for the sake of Christ, because when I'm weak, then I'm strong." My Nan exemplified strength, grace and dignity that could speak, not despite her disability, but rather, was all the more impressive in the face of it.

Having live-in grandparents was not always easy. There was a constant stream of caretakers ("the helpers" we called them) walking in and out of our house—some of them good and loving, others manipulative and dishonest. There was an ever-present threat of financial collapse—the weight of caring for a seven-person household falling heavily on two parents who worked in helping professions with limited income advancement. Though we had moved into this enormous house, my grandparents lived in a small portion of it—a bedroom off of the dining room of the house, with a handicap accessible bathroom attached, added especially for them. They would spread out a little during the day, but mostly stayed in their "apartment." Despite working so very hard to take up as little space as possible, their presence permeated the experience of every member of the household in ways that were both good and challenging. As I got older, there were times when I resented not being able to simply be alone at my house and always feeling obligated to spend time with them. This is to say nothing of the individual hardships and heartaches that each member of the household experienced by this cohabitation.

Yet of all the people in our household, I benefited the most from their presence. Of all of my siblings, I spent the most time with my grandparents. I was only two when they arrived and my siblings were already launched into the world when my grandfather died my sophomore year of high school and when my grandma died when I was a junior in college.

Many of the memories of my life are filled with them and there is a direct line between my profession, who I was shaped to be in the world, and my grandparents.

My Grampy died when I was seventeen. My dad came and picked me up from school after it happened and when I ran into the house to find my Nan, I burst into the kitchen and through the bathroom where I stopped because there he lay, his body still warm, the paramedics still packing up their things, everyone awaiting the arrival of the funeral home. I remember laying down on the floor with him, putting my head on his chest, something I hadn't been able to do for years because of his frailty.

In the weeks before my Nan died, she was in the hospital. She had stopped eating, she had been unconscious for days and I came home every weekend to see her, feeling the looming loss of her deeply. On my last visit before she died, I combed her hair and put lotion on her hands. We were alone and so I took her hand in mine and laid my head on her lap and cried. As I was weeping, she squeezed my hand. Her hand and arm, which for the last forty-five years had been devoid of any feeling or ability to move due to paralysis caused by MS, squeezed my hand. I left that day confounded and comforted.

There is deep pain in these losses, but there is also profound and inexplicable comfort. In the hardest moments, I was gifted not with what I wanted, but with what I needed.

It was late on a Saturday evening when I received the call that a parishioner, Ward, was near death and my presence was requested. I was home alone with six-month-old Liam; Alan and Sam off on a weekend adventure. My parents were over an hour away. I panicked. It was ten o'clock at night—time was of the essence—who in the world could I hand this baby over to so that I could be by the side of the family as they bid farewell to their loved one? There were just no options. He had to come with me, but it was an incredible gamble. He was fast asleep as I tucked him into his carrier, blankets tucked around him to protect him from the cold.

What if he woke up and started screaming? What if they were deep in grief and angry that it took me so long to get there and I show up with a baby? What if I was not able to be present to the family in the way that is required? For all we celebrate of motherhood, culturally we are ruthless when a woman can't juggle it all. We criticize her if she is too committed to her job, while also slamming her if she is too focused on her children. There is so little grace. And though this family is genuine, warm, caring... they were deep in grief. Bringing a baby to that grief is not exactly pastoral excellence. But here we were, and I had to do it.

I entered the apartment and gently put sleeping Liam down in the living room, tentatively taking steps into the bedroom where the family was perched. As they parted the circle around Ward to make room for my presence, his wife said, "you just missed it... he's gone."

There are many times when I feel like an utter failure in ministry, when who I am and what I bring to the table are simply not equal to the task in front of me. Doubt of oneself feels to be, at least a little bit, knit into the consciousness of every pastor I know. It's moments like this that we fear. Times where we miss the critical moment or make the wrong decision. We forget (at least for a time) that the story is so much bigger than what we do. That no one moment or decision defines a ministry. Hell, we forget that maybe we just aren't that important. We lose sight of all that and become hyper focused on whether or not we are who others need us to be. Because of that, this memory from early in my ministry is seared into my consciousness. The memory of how shattered and overwhelmed I was with that chasm of impossibility that is being a working mother. I couldn't leave my baby, and I had to go to the bedside. In the end, I feared that I failed at both.

Of course, I said none of this. I simply did what we do: I met them where they were and offered the pastoral care that I could with what I had. We closed the circle again and prayed together, blessing Ward on his journey to God, and requesting comfort and peace for his family. At the Amen, there was a stirring—the rustling of blankets and the soft mewl of baby Liam. We looked at one another and I said, "I'm sorry, I had to bring Liam, no one else is home right now."

One thing that is true of Liam, even to this day, is that really, his favorite place to be is beside me. When he was a baby, if he could be near me, could smell me and be held by me, all would be well. I stepped out of the room and picked him up out of the carrier, his eyes sleepy and unfocused. I swaddled him in the blanket and carried him back into the room, already back asleep in the comfort of my arms. We all sat down around Ward's bed, Liam in my arms and the family looking on.

I was ashamed. Would they report this unprofessionalism? Would they send me away in the name of being a good mother? Would they remind me of my weakness? But there was none of that. They greeted me and Liam with such openness and compassion, but perhaps most surprisingly, they greeted me with gratitude. One by one, they gazed at Liam and felt the soft hair on his head. They rubbed his fat, pink cheeks with their knuckles and laughed when he sneezed in his sleep.

"Can I... can I hold him, Danielle?" Ward's son asked. Yes, of course.

"My dad... he just died... and here Liam is... so full of life. It really is... what we need."

And there it was again—strength made perfect from weakness, from vulnerability, from heartache. There are many, many times (maybe always?), when I am a shadow of who I think I need to be. There are many times (perhaps every time?) when I can only bring what I have to give in the moment and pray that it's enough. Sometimes, I fall on my face. I forget the sister's name in the middle of the prayer, or I completely flub up a reference to a biblical story, or I spew some cheap platitude of comfort instead of sitting quietly alongside someone in deep pain. But sometimes. Sometimes, the table of circumstances that have been laid out seem completely incongruous, with no possible room for grace, and yet the imperfect variables come together and grace finds a seat at that table. As though it were meant to be set that way all along. As though the weakness brought forth was just what the moment needed, and what is revealed is the strength of God.

BRIMMING WITH THE SACRED

Jessie

I am sitting in a sunny kitchen in Rye, New York. A man in his eighties sits on the counter top, his lanky, khaki-ed legs hooked at the ankles. As he leans forward, both hands on either side of his hips, he explains, "Everything is slower now. I don't feel the old pressure to hurry or get it right or get it done. Which means it's weirder. Slower, weirder, and infinitely more pleasurable."

We are talking about sex.

I am interviewing senior citizens about their sex lives and sensual identities. I wrote a proposal to explore this subject and this earned me a commission, my largest yet, to write a play about the sex lives of seniors. Since I am not a senior (yet!), I am interviewing as many as I can, and what I discover is far from the shyness or reserve with which I know this generation was raised around sex. They are *frank*. And funny! They are honest, introspective, and adventurous.

Like the woman in Denver, Colorado, who orders our appetizers and launches: "I've decided to resuscitate my sex life. Literally. I'm bringing it back from the dead."

I ask her what "the dead" means for her.

"I was married to a man for twenty-five years," she replies. "I had to submit to him sexually. I didn't like it. Now I'm ready to try things on my terms." She is seventy-five, with an angular nose and sharp dark eyes. When I ask what happened to that husband she flatly replies, "He died, thank God," and sips her iced tea.

This is what it is to be a writer in the world. Your curiosity is your compass. Of course, everyone can do this, one needn't be a writer, but few people do. Being a writer means you can ask incredibly intimate questions and then add, "I'm a writer" and it's okay. It's like showing your badge. It says: *This is for my work. This is to make story.* People open up.

Like the little museum guard in the National Gallery in London a few years ago.

I was standing in front of a large painting with my hands on my heart. Tears streamed down my face. This is a little embarrassing to admit now, but I was moved by the painting. The subject was a woman. She had blond hair and pale skin with rosy cheeks; her hips were round with a layer of fat that encircled her belly, her arms and back. *She looked like me.* This simple realization made me think about how important it is to see ourselves in art. To have heroes and heroines who match what we see in the mirror. To hear our pronoun in the sacred texts. We need to see and hear ourselves to be assured that the sacred includes us. Directly, unequivocally, no transcription necessary.

I was thinking all this when I looked beside me and suddenly noticed the museum guard, a small man, sitting in a chair just a few feet away. He had wisps of strawberry hair around his shiny bald scalp. Mischievous eyes twinkled out from little spectacles. I was struck that this man watched this art all day long. But he also watched those of us who came to see it. Then, because I am a writer, I asked him *what that was like.* By the end of a year, I had interviewed over thirty museum guards. London, Washington, DC, New York. I wanted to know how they came to that job, what they loved about it, what people don't realize about their job, what room in the museum they enjoyed most ("The Dutch interiors," by the way, is the answer from an uncanny number of museum guards). All this inspired my play *The Rembrandt*, about a museum guard who decides to deliberately touch a famous Rembrandt painting and how that changes him. These interviews with museum guards, often next to great works of art, made me think about the ephemeral and the eternal: How a great work of art can endure but a human being will pass, and how there are only one of each in all of time. One *Aristotle with a Bust of Homer*, one *Starry Night*. One you. One me.

Writing has brought many gifts like this.

Sitting in the National Library in Florence, Italy, after hours of cajoling guards and librarians to let me deeper into the archives, in front of the original letters from Galileo Galilei's eldest daughter. She was his confidant and best friend. She was also his real estate agent and defendant, lobbying his powerful friends to help against the Inquisition that threatened to torture him for his assertion that the earth rotated around the sun. All from a convent. She wrote him every day, and one hundred and twenty-four letters survive. I touched the parchment, tracing the delicate embellishments of her handwriting as she beseeches him to rest, to be gentle with himself, to try to live (even though she herself would die terribly young).

Or sitting in a sun-drenched office in Princeton, New Jersey, with a young physicist considered the brightest of his generation. He is describing in equal detail the perfection of the laws of our universe and the perfection of his beloved cat Tempest. He considers himself an atheist, but also deliberately and lovingly embraces spiritual terms to communicate the elegance of the laws of physics. "As far as modern physics has come," he muses mischievously, "We are not even close to understanding the nature of human consciousness."

Or sweating heavily from a run in Brussels, looking up at the house where Bruegel the Elder, the famous Flemish painter, lived until his death in 1569, only to see the front door open and a workman step out for a cigarette. Long, thoughtful wrinkles stretched from the top of his brow, down around his chin. I stand there for a moment, amazed at my luck, and then walk over and introduce myself. He is there to renovate the woodwork inside the home in preparation for it to become a museum. Today is his last day. I tell him I am a writer and ask if I can come inside. He cocks his head, considering me, then says yes.

I believe everyone can write. Not that everyone is meant to be a writer. It is a craft and it is difficult and it takes a lot of work to be good at it. But everyone is in the middle of their life and has profound realizations and memories and stories inside them. This is the sacred inside of us. It deserves to be heard. It deserves to be written down. To be a writer is to experience the immense privilege of hearing someone else's truth, mingling it with your own, and sharing it with others. In the face of societal indifference, violence and prejudice and alienation, what could be more worthwhile?

Benedictions ❀ 173

But most of the time, I don't feel like I am illuminating the sacred. When I am slogging away on the four hundred and twenty-ninth rewrite, I feel tired and mediocre. I feel petty and anxious. I don't travel the world and interview people about intimate subjects because I am called to illuminate the sacred. I do it because I really, really like it. Do I *hope* something I write will do good? Absolutely. Do I write *because* it will do good? Absolutely not. I write because it endlessly interests me. It pleases me. I write because I can't *not* write. If you were to lock me in a room without my journal and pen, I would find a rock on the ground. I would start scratching on the walls.

Dani and I talk on the phone at eight o'clock almost every weekday morning. We are in the middle of our morning routines, which means she is heading to the church, and I am drinking coffee and journaling in my pajamas. Now that I live in France, this is just after lunch. This phone call is like our power meeting: We cover what we're feeling, daily life stuff (our worries, our complaints, our outfits), and then we move to our work for the day.

My report is usually something like this: "I got the network's notes on my pilot so I'm going to work on those. Then I want to do a long hike. Then I have a call for the movie thing and I want to re-read the play for the upcoming workshop and make a work list. Then I'm making a new recipe from the *New York Times* of an Iranian stew for dinner."

Dani's report is usually something like this: "Remember that parishioner that had the weird liver thing last month? They have a big surgery today so I'm going to the hospital for that, then I promised another parishioner who was recently widowed I'd have lunch with them; then I'm meeting a couple that's dealing with an affair, then I have a meeting to find community partners for this charity I'm leading. Liam had a bad dream last night so I want to pick up a special night light for his room, we have a teleconference with Gracie's doctor, Sam has Scouts" and then she might have three meetings in the evening about poverty.

I think you know where I'm going with this.

Dani's life makes other people's lives better. Directly. Mine is just good for me. Basically.

Not that Dani would agree. She sees the highest aim in what I'm trying to do. And she often reminds me. Connects me to that far away moment when maybe something I've written will go into the world. It will move someone to consider their life a little differently. With more tenderness and care. With more wonder. More joy. By recording the details of the beautiful world around us and the truths of the people in it, it's less easy to drop a bomb on it all. It's less easy to submit to despair and cruelty. The world and all the people in it are revealed for what they truly are—brimming with story. Brimming with the sacred.

PINEAPPLE MAN

Dani

Gregory came to church every Sunday. He sat three-quarters of the way back on the right side of the sanctuary, along the center aisle. He had a sort of droopy face, like one of those faces that had a perpetual sadness to it—but Gregory wasn't a sad man. I started visiting Gregory because he lived just a few blocks from church at the top of a hill and he had commented to me, on more than one occasion, that he wanted me to come see his garden. Visitation is one of the most difficult parts about pastoring—at least I think so. It is one of those things that never leaves the to-do list. The list of who to visit literally never runs out and time always does.

Every week, I feel this awful tension—who is homebound that needs to be visited, who is going through a difficult time that needs to be called, who is in the hospital that needs to be visited, what nursing home needs a check in, and who is lonely. That is just who is on the list—it says nothing of the folks who call because something has come up, or text, or stop in. It says nothing of the freezer breaking down and needing to clean out its contents. It says nothing of the sermon needing to be written, or the stream of meetings to attend, or the planning and preparing and setting up. It's the best and hardest thing about being a pastor—the smorgasbord of what might make up your day. And so visitation sits like a stone for me because I never feel like it's enough and I *know* it isn't enough. Someone is always disappointed.

So when Gregory invites me over every Sunday, it's rough because as far as I can see and know, Gregory is doing okay. He's old (in his nineties), but he's not infirmed. He lives alone, but he's not without family. He is slow, but he can still drive and go to restaurants. He's not one of the people that will make the list, and that's not because I don't want to spend time with Gregory, it's because of all the things I listed above. But when people ask, I genuinely try to say yes. To find a way to stop in and visit. So, every couple of months, I find a way to visit Gregory.

The first time I visited him, it was the summer and we walked around the yard. He lived in a rancher with a patio that looked out on his backyard which had a small patch of flat land, then a steep incline that rose to a tree line. Along that hill was a large, fenced in garden. As we're walking up the hill to the garden, Gregory stops at a few small trees about halfway up. From a distance, they look like normal trees, sort of like crabapple trees; but when you get up close there are two trunks—they're distinct, but they're also together. He explains to me that these are two apple trees that have been grafted together. In many ways they are two distinct trees, with individual trunks, but at some point they grew together and their branches intertwined, and there is no way to tell them apart except that some branches grow gala and some grow fuji. Gregory is a master gardener. I mean, I know that's a real title, and I don't know if he earned that title in a competition or anything, but it's clear: Gregory knows what he's doing.

We walk further up the lawn to the fenced in garden and there are many, many plants growing there. He smiles with pride. Behind the fenced area are huge plastic barrels of lots of different colors that have tubing coming out of them. There is no way that I can do it justice to describe it, but Gregory had engineered an irrigation system. He had designed it, found and adapted the items to be able to build it, and then installed it. It was a marvel. "I just hated climbing up this hill all the time with a hose . . . so I decided to make it so I didn't have to."

And then behind all of that, was a little shed, where he kept his mini tractor/riding mower. He showed me how he rode around on the yard, with the tractor teetering at precarious angles on the hill.

When we finally settle back down at the patio to have some lemonade, we sit in the chairs and look out at everything and off to the right on the patio is a giant potted plant. I go over to it and ask, "What is this one, Gregory?"

"That's my pineapple plant." And he laughs. "It's never once given me a pineapple. I can't seem to grow a pineapple. I keep it around though—it's a good reminder—I can't grow everything."

This master gardener, this genius of cultivating growth, couldn't grow a pineapple. He'd had that plant for twenty years.

And with Gregory's vast talent, with his incredible history of intuitively understanding how to grow things, it struck me that in this paradise, amidst this Eden-like example of his expertise, a lone pineapple plant held the place of honor. A pot on the patio, beside Gregory's favorite chair. Gregory held that failure of a plant with such regard and kindness. When talking about the pineapple plant, he neither disparaged his own skills nor blamed the plant. And when determining what to do with it, he didn't throw it out or hide it with other, more triumphant plants. No, he just let it have its place on his patio. He went ahead and let his heart hang on this little plant that wouldn't grow, a thing of pride where others would find embarrassment.

It was another year or two later when Gregory made the difficult decision to move into a nursing home, to leave the acres he had tended, the land where he had labored faithfully. The pineapple plant was the only plant he brought with him.

Not everything we intend—not everything we nurture—comes to fruition. There's a parable about that. This gardener sows seed recklessly, with abandon, all over different types of land and soil. Some of the seeds don't even last long enough to take root—they're swept away by wind or the birds eat them. Other seeds take root, but not deep enough and so can't ever really grow, or they take root but are scorched by the sun or drowned by the rain. But there are some seeds that seem to click into place and the plant grows and flourishes. There's a parable that says that.

But there isn't a parable for the plant that is loved and cared for...the plant that is nourished and tended but just never bears fruit. There's no parable for that but I think it's as true a story—as true an outcome—as any. Gregory taught me about tending the things that don't bear fruit. He got me considering—is there a way to hold with tenderness the paths not taken or the futures we hoped for that never came to fruition? Gregory kept that plant on the patio and he took that plant to the nursing home as a reminder: we can't grow everything. Not everything we tend will bloom. And yet still it deserves tending, maybe even deserves to be held in esteem.

The life of an artist is testimony to this. Growing up in Waynesboro, our little hometown in south central Pennsylvania, Jessie was a big fish in a little pond. Her talent was apparent from a very early age. For however she felt inside, Jessie presented as self-assured, gregarious, and outgoing. She was also mature beyond her years and emo without the ennui. She just felt things deeply and had a way of communicating those things in writing, in song, in acting. Of course, this meant I idolized her. I tried to be good at all the same things and was only half as successful. And I don't say that to insinuate that I suck. I say it because she was just that extraordinary and this is what it meant to follow in the footsteps of a sibling who was extraordinary. Every talent or gift or aptitude is seen in comparison. I remember in the seventh grade, I was asked to sing a song for the school concert and when I balked at such a responsibility, the teacher matter-of-factly looked me up and down and said, "If you're anything like your sister, you'll do it."

In the end, I found my own measure of success in the pond of Waynesboro, but the truth is, the things that I cultivated there, for the most part, were the plantings of my sister. They were plants that I might get to grow but would never be the things that would bear fruit in my life—but I'm glad I tended them. I'm glad that I tended theater and music because I found community in those things, and ultimately, it was theater and music that would help guide me back to church.

Growing up as a performer and living a life as a professional artist are two very different things. Over the last twenty-four years since Jessie left Waynesboro, I have watched her tend many plants that never bloomed. I've watched her cultivate and nurture many parts and plays and scripts that would never bear fruit. To be a professional artist is to tend an entire field, labor in an entire field, and never know if your labors will be realized. You never know if your labor will translate into something that can actually buy you groceries and pay your rent.

As an observer of the art Jessie has participated in and created herself over the last twenty-four years, I have never once wondered if what she was tending was worth it. I could see—regardless of the success of any one project or play—that the gift of theater is that it gives voice to experiences; it gives common language to what it means to live in the world; and it often gives voice to a perspective that is not my own, to experiences to which I cannot relate but can understand because it points to something true within myself.

The constant shadow that follows me in my life as a pastor is the question, "Will anything that I have tended, anything I have planted matter or grow? And how would I know if they did?" What does the landscape of a field well-tended in ministry even look like? As I prepare the list for visitation, or sit down to write a sermon, or make phone calls to find volunteers, or cut one hundred strips of paper for a craft or any of the other seemingly Sisyphean tasks of ministry—will there be fruits of that labor, or will the only thing that follows me be monikers of tepidness, "Pastor Dani—sometimes visited." "Pastor Dani—world's okayest preacher." "Pastor Dani—went to meetings."

When I look on the landscape of ministry, there are precious few moments where I can look and say, "Look what I planted" or "Look what I grew." There are frighteningly few moments where I know with certainty that my presence or what I did mattered. So few. So few that it almost feels futile, hopeless, even stupid to have tried. Except...except that God is rarely in prize-winning plants. God is rarely in the biggest and brightest blooms. And ministry is rarely about anything that any one of us does alone. Though God certainly can be seen in the exceptional, I've found that God is most often in the mundane, in the simple, in the everyday, slow, and persistent work of tending and nurturing. God is most often in the pineapple plant that doesn't grow—but teaches us about the sure and steady work of tending and nurturing, the sure and steady work of love for Love's sake.

WHAT IF WE GET CANCER (AND OTHER POSSIBLE ENDINGS)

Jessie

I remember there were scissors.

We were playing on my parents' bed. Dani was maybe six, which would've made me eight or nine. And somehow things turned fire-y. Nerve-y. The way animals wrestling is fun and playful. Until it isn't.

Suddenly Dani was holding the scissors, open, poised over the soft stretchy tissue between my thumb and my pointer finger. I dared her. She waited. Then a glint across her bright blue eyes. And she cut.

The scar is still there. Shiny, subtle. I remember being shocked she did it. And also glad. Maybe I had already started to fear I really was The Bad One. Dani was The

Good One. Letting me make the mistakes, zoom ahead, fall down, fail, laugh too loud, cuss too much, want too much, risk too much, definitely say too much. And at the same time—somewhere deep down, I think she cut me because I wanted her to. She sensed it. The power of being the younger in a dyad is the pressure to keep up. And the example to follow. The only way to stay close to your older sibling, if they'll let you, is to do just that—stay close. Keep functioning up. Keep cultivating the humor, the insights, the games, the maturity. I see it in my brother's daughters now. The older sibling is trying to individuate and make her way while still keeping the younger sibling close and safe; the younger sibling is trying to keep up, keep relevant, while still carving out her own identity and power.

Something that's changed in middle age is my relationship to worry. I sometimes find myself up at night going over the party conversation. The changes in the world and my place in it. Trying to see into a crystal ball how the landscape of my life has changed, how it might continue changing. I've never been a big worrier. Because I was *young*. I knew I had time. Time to make my career, to make money, to learn what the fuck an IRA is and get one. Time to buy a house. Time to build safety nets.

But now I'm at the beginning of middle age. And wow is that shit real. I have fears. Rattle-y-around-y fears. Like what if my freelance work dries up? What if I age out of my field and haven't built enough retirement? What if I die like Rembrandt, diseased, destitute, and alone?

What if I get cancer?

Or glaucoma. Or dementia. Or Alzheimer's. Or multiple sclerosis. Or some other horror whose name I've no reason to know yet.

What if Dani does?

This is my number one fear: That Dani will die and her children will have to grow up without her. Those of us left behind, who love her and know *exactly* how beautifully she mothered them, will have to approximate her unique care and know how poor we are in comparison. We'll look into the beautiful blue eyes of all three of her children and think, "Sorry little buddy. Your mommy was the best and you're stuck with the B team."

The process of writing this book has illuminated that we are in a moment in time. Dani is deep in the trenches of raising three children. Leading a thriving church community. Happily married. I am in a period of freedom. A little more financially stable. Employed with cool contracts. Settled in France with my partner. Here we are. Writing about how we are who we are. Writing about the past. Not knowing the future. Perhaps there will be a sequel. When we have faced disease. And loss. When we'll have buried our parents. Or each other. I prefer not to think about it.

I prefer to think ahead. Two jolly old ladies. Happy and a little fat. Wrinkly. Laughing. Irreverent. Red cheeked. Sitting on a porch. Two rocking chairs. With enormous cushions for our enormous butts. Arm rests. Side tables perfectly placed to hold our drinks. Me: daytime seltzer, evening wine. Dani: Coke all the time.

Talking about the past. Remembering the way our parents were, realizing new things about them, the dynamics of our family, the specters of our childhood. Analyzing the television shows we're watching. The books we're reading.

Dani will wear cute old lady accoutrement. T-shirts with flowers or butterflies. Pastel cardigans. Big necklaces with matching earrings. Elastic waist pants. I too will wear elastic waist pants. Fitted pants will in fact be banned. But I'll still own a blazer. Or cardigans shaped like a blazer. Lower necklines. A few designer pieces tucked in there. Her hair will still be an adorable, manicured bob. Mine will still be an untamed, blond nest. I'll still exercise every day. Long walks and hikes. Maybe by then I'll have added senior-y exercise like water aerobics. Dani will still prefer to stay home and read. Cook dinner. She'll still do little hump-y dances when she's pleased. I'll still do character-y voices and jokes. We'll still laugh so hard it turns into nonsensical high-pitched keening, when the words become unintelligible and your eyes are watering and you know you're out of control now and that makes it all the funnier.

She'll still bring up how I made her smell my feet and told her they smelled like cherry pie. I'll still remind her that she believed me every time. Our periods will be ancient history. As will our knees. And our boobs.

I once heard Dani preach about the kingdom of heaven. Jesus begins each parable with the refrain "The Kingdom of Heaven is like..." He then goes on to describe a scene from regular life that also describes the afterlife.

Not very clear? Let me elucidate:

An example of a parable (paraphrased): The kingdom of heaven is like a farmer planting wheat and then his enemy planting weeds, but the farmer tells his workers to let them both grow together. Until the harvest. Then the weeds should be pulled and burned, and then the wheat should be gathered and stored.

Another example: The kingdom of heaven is like a treasure hidden in a field. When the man found it, he was so overjoyed that he reburied the treasure, sold everything he had, and bought that field.

Another example: The kingdom of heaven is like a woman putting yeast in the dough and spreading it around.

Still not clear?

EXACTLY.

Oh, Bible. I have notes for you! *Notes*.

But I like the refrain—"The kingdom of heaven is like..." And it's been circling in my mind as we write this book. Particularly now that I find myself gazing forward, squinting into the future.

The kingdom of heaven is like a Coca-Cola tea party.

It's popcorn, milkduds, and Coke. (Or popcornmilkdudsandcoke.)

The kingdom of heaven is trying to steal a road sign in the middle of the night.

It's wildflowers and cut grass inside a picket fence.

It's two nitzes in a couch fort.

It's one badass lady. With two broke ovaries.

It's a phone call unanswered.

It's rage newly found.

It's a room full of people listening to a story in the dark.

It's a pineapple plant that doesn't bloom.

It's stolen t-shirts and flower hospitals.

It's leavings that are actually beginnings.

It's birthing babies. And midwifing alongside.

It's living apart. And letting go.

The kingdom of heaven is anything this long life gives us. And the people who archive it with us. Sisters and husbands. Friends and family. Who remind us when we forget.

It's death beds. And funeral processions. And long drives. And benedictions.

The kingdom of heaven is here inside us.

Mirrored by the ones we love.

BENEDICTIONS

Dani

At the end of every worship service, there is a benediction—a word of blessing.

It's the precious pause where we hold tight a little longer to the sacred thing that happened here, and then the gentle opening to what will come next, to what is ahead.

Jessie said early on that this book is a heart space. I think it's a benediction.

We are capturing, treasuring, archiving what has been these last forty years—and turning to face the sun.

Because in truth, my sistering with Jessie is changing. It was never about proximity (since leaving for college, we haven't lived close to each other), but the familiarity with which I understand her life is shifting.

First of all, she speaks French now. She would say she is shit at it, but she's wrong. She has worked hard to be able to communicate in the country where she now finds her home. And I guess that's the other thing: she calls somewhere else home and it bears little relationship to me.

I used to take great comfort in knowing that at any moment, I could get to Jessie in a matter of hours—or she could get to me. I could locate in my mental map what stationery store she was calling me from in Brooklyn. When she would tell me who she was meeting for dinner, I knew them.

Now, she hikes in mountains that are unfamiliar. She drinks wine from a vineyard a few kilometers away. She eats dinner at nine o'clock in the evening! She is blissfully, unfathomably happy.

Of course, these things say nothing about who she is internally—but somehow they do. They tell me about experiences that I haven't had or relationships that I haven't been around to see grow. If a benediction is a sending forth—she has been sent forth and sometimes it feels like I'm still waiting in the sanctuary.

I'm currently in the trenches and they are trenches that I have chosen and would choose again one hundred times. I am parenting three kids, spanning the life stages from toddler to adolescent. My days are a constant cycle of getting little people ready for things, then going to work and spiritually mothering a church, then coming home and making dinner, then attending some meetings, then putting little people to bed, then reading a book until it falls on my face because I can't keep my eyes open. I'm married to a man and we've been together longer than we've been apart. It sounds like a slog—and it is—but it is also deeply fulfilling and sometimes I can't breathe, I feel so lucky.

But those are different lives, right? More different than they've ever been. And it's hard to know what the future looks like. In my worst moments, because I can be selfish, I only think about what I've lost:

Instead of seeing my sister every few months, I now can only afford to see her once a year.

Instead of her getting the slow and steady progression of my children's development, she'll experience it in leaps.

Instead of knowing each of her friends, I'll have to settle for hearing about them.

I've cried about these losses in moments of self-pity.

But even this loss is a benediction—an exhale of grief before an inhale of possibility. And I know that there is possibility; there is more to our sistering.

I know this because this most recent divergence in our sistering was born out of a time of remarkable growth and self-determination in Jessie's life. Seeing that unfold and witnessing where she is now prevents me from spending too long in wistfulness for the past. And besides this, I am a person of faith. I worry constantly about money, about childcare, about what to make for dinner, about parishioners, about whether or not I need to change the oil in my car—but I don't worry about the future. I don't worry about whether or not it will be alright.

It will.

I don't worry about whether Jessie and I will keep sistering.

We will.

And so, I look back on this time and reflect on its goodness. I take the precious pause intrinsic in benedictions and then I turn myself around, take her hand and walk towards what is next.